FIGHTING TODAY'S WARS

How America's Leaders Have
Failed Our Warriors

DAVID G. BOLGIANO
and
JAMES M. PATTERSON

STACKPOLE
BOOKS

For Christian, Daniel, and Maggie Bolgiano
and Jimmy and Ashley Patterson

"If there must be trouble, let it be in my day, that my child
may have peace."—*Tom Paine, 1776*

Copyright © 2012 by Stackpole Books

Published by
STACKPOLE BOOKS
5067 Ritter Road
Mechanicsburg, PA 17055
www.stackpolebooks.com

Printed in the United States of America

First edition

10 9 8 7 6 5 4 3 2 1

Library of Congress Cataloging-in-Publication Data

Bolgiano, David G.
   Fighting today's wars: how America's leaders have failed our warriors /
David G. Bolgiano and James M. Patterson. — 1st ed.
      p. cm.
   Includes bibliographical references.
   ISBN-13: 978-0-8117-0776-3 (hardcover)
   ISBN-10: 0-8117-0776-8 (hardcover)
   1. Military law—United States. 2. United States—Armed Forces—
Regulations. I. Patterson, James M. (James Michael), 1961– II. Title.
   KF7209.B65 2012
   343.73'01—dc23
                              2011033763

CONTENTS

FOREWORD

The well-trained and dominant American warfighting force of the Reagan era is gone. Over the last two decades the unparalleled military of the 1980s has been systematically eroded by an incessant wave of politically influenced thought on how we should wage war. *Fighting Today's Wars* is a startling look at this insidious slide of our armed forces from a position of readiness to a position of timidity and avoidance. Today our newly transformed "full spectrum operations" force trains more on stability operations and nation-building tasks than on the warfighting mission for which it was conceived. As a result, thousands of our best and brightest have died on faraway battlefields in the last ten years; principled, properly focused leadership could have saved many of these patriots.

In June 2011, two Iraqi men living in Kentucky were arrested and charged with conspiracy to kill a United States national, conspiracy to use a weapon of mass destruction, attempting to provide material support to terrorists, and knowingly transferring a device designed to launch a missile. A year earlier, the FBI had begun contacting numerous leaders of the brigade that I commanded in Iraq in 2005 and 2006. These inquiries informed a feverish search by the Department of Justice to locate several dozen Iraqi insurgents who had been granted visas by the Department of State. These enemy combatants were granted refugee status after they were released from American detention cells in Iraq following a directive from the senior operational commander implementing unrealistic evidentiary requirements for incarceration. At least one of the men apprehended in Kentucky had been arrested by our unit while in Iraq, but he was subsequently released due to the new, softer detention policy.

It's instructive to review this Iraqi's activities over the twelve months he was in the United States. When he was not serving as the front man for al Qaeda in the acquisition and transportation of weapons and munitions back to Iraq, he spent much of his time actively searching for one of the brigade's subordinate commanders; his intention was to assassinate this American army officer on American soil. The new policy stipulating a nearly unachievable standard for evidence collection, the policy directly responsible for this incident, was mockingly called the "catch-and-release program" by combat soldiers. This uninformed guidance led to the number of enemy detainees during operations dropping precipitously, and the majority of enemy combatants already incarcerated were unceremoniously released back into the general population. The result was predictable: American soldiers died, and others were maimed for life. And now, six years later, one of the negative effects of this politically motivated decision is that al Qaeda operatives, men directly culpable or complicit in the death of Americans, are roaming the streets of America with impunity while they actively support the war in Iraq against America.

In my frequent discussions with junior leaders, I am often struck by the clarity of their observations and opinions of our institution's leadership. I recently spoke to a disheartened young man who confided that his best friend and fellow soldier was killed in Iraq because he hesitated when an insurgent presented a clear lethal threat to his unit. The hesitation, according to this young sergeant, was not due to fear or his inability to respond, but rather was a result of his haunting fear of legal reprisal. The two had engaged in frequent discussions on the witch hunt that followed any engagement, regardless of the legality or necessity of the incident. Don't miss this point—at the moment of truth, rather than being focused on killing enemy combatants and keeping their soldiers alive, junior leaders are preoccupied with surviving the legal aftermath orchestrated by the senior leaders in their chain of command. This notion is reinforced by several young company commanders who told about improvements needed in the curriculum of our professional education courses—alarmingly, the number one recommendation was to add a course to teach leaders how to survive a Criminal Investigation Division (CID) post-incident interview.

How does this happen? How do American soldiers find themselves in a combat zone and torn between responding quickly and appropriately to the enemy and protecting themselves from the threat of an unsympathetic and career-ending investigation by the CID? Why are our units hesitating before they engage an enemy who's trying to kill them—or in some cases, taking extreme measures to avoid confrontation with a poorly trained, equipped, and led group of rag-tag insurgents that even a poorly trained American unit could quickly overwhelm? Why are senior commanders giving rewards to units that capture insurgents rather than kill them?

These questions are precisely those which Jim Patterson and David "Bo" Bolgiano pose and eruditely answer in this book. Admittedly their analysis is blunt and hard to stomach—yet our ten-year history in Iraq and Afghanistan corroborates their position. Whether you are a seasoned combat veteran who can empathize with the numerous challenges our troops face due to politically minded leadership, or you have no military experience and are uninformed on the contemptuous manner in which we're treating those doing the nation's fighting . . . regardless of your experience and knowledge, this book is one you need to read.

This is truly a rare work—partly because it directly confronts the risk-averse senior leaders of our military institution, and maybe more importantly because it comes from the unique perspective of military lawyers. It is quite possibly the first work of its kind, as most staff judge advocates are reluctant to take a definitive position, particularly when it comes to rules of engagement and operations in a combat zone. Jim and Bo not only identify the problem, they follow up their observations and insights with constructive recommendations on how we can win in war and restore the trust and confidence of our soldiers in their leaders.

Bo has carried an added burden throughout the writing of this book. Midway through the writing, he was diagnosed with metastatic melanoma. Yet his driving commitment throughout his treatment has been to get this book published and into the hands of those who need to be informed of our army's current lamentable condition. Completing this book has been Bo's singular focus.

The compulsion to make a difference has led Jim and Bo to generously donate a significant portion of the proceeds from this book to support those service members who have been wounded in action—proceeds that will assist with their treatment and recovery. Bo and Jim will donate a portion of their royalties to the Faces of Freedom, a nonprofit veterans' support organization founded in 2009. The Faces of Freedom assists returning wounded veterans and their families whatever their needs—mental, emotional, physical, financial, or spiritual. The program is built on developing personal relationships with each veteran and begins with extensive coaching to help the wounded veterans reintegrate with society and family and then prepares them with counseling and mentoring skills to counsel the next wave of returning wounded troops. More information on the Faces of Freedom and how you can support these efforts can be found at facesoffreedomgeorgia.com.

Illuminating the condition of our armed forces is long overdue, and I'm proud that two friends, both superb soldiers and military lawyers, have the courage to be the forerunners on this issue. Their book is a truly meaningful work that should be read by every senior military leader, every elected official, and the families of every service member. America can rearm its soldiers with policies and rules of engagement that safeguard our heroes and enable them to accomplish their mission and return home victorious.

—Colonel Michael Steele
USA, Retired

PREFACE

Late on a fall night in 1980, a small team of specialists silently slipped through the brush. At 2200 hours the soldiers hit their objective rally point (ORP) and dropped their rucksacks. Stripping down to combat essentials, they splintered off in different directions to accomplish the mission: destroying a small bridge controlling a key sanctuary for enemy rebels. Taking out the bridge would isolate the guerrillas and buy time for the beleaguered government to marshal its forces. This was typical direct action supporting a foreign internal defense mission. The problem was that the bridge was guarded by an elite cadre of the guerrillas' most experienced fighters. Prior attempts by the government to infiltrate the area and isolate the guerrillas had not been successful.

I and eleven other young troops in the chill of night stealthily approached the guerillas' strongpoint. Despite the cool autumn air, I was sweating through my camouflage face paint. The night conditions were perfect: illumination at 17 percent; leaves and brush soft with recent rain; and so dark you couldn't see your hand in front of your face. I followed the phosphorescent "cat-eyes" sewn onto the back of the patrol cap on the soldier in front of me. I tapped my partner on the shoulder to adjust his direction as I stayed focused on the illuminated tritium dial of my compass. After what seemed an interminable approach, we hit the stream juncture that we were using as a checkpoint for our entrance into our support position. We had to have our machine gun in position and ready to fire at exactly 2400 hours. After slowing to scoop up a canteen of cold water from the stream, we turned 90 degrees and started the slight climb to a previously reconnoitered position. The position was slightly elevated and had a clear field of fire onto the bridge and surrounding environs. The brush in that sector was sufficiently sparse to allow for a good beaten zone.

We eased into position and I checked my watch—2347 hours. In thirteen minutes, two machine guns would pour fire on the exposed sentries. Nearing midnight, the rebels showed their typical disdain for security; a medium fire burning off to the side of the bridge illuminated the rebel guards, who were either busy eating or curled up in their sleeping bags. Not one had his weapon at the ready nor did there appear to be any security patrols ranging from the bridge.

At precisely 2400 hours, I slapped the gunner on the head, signaling him to cut loose with a lengthy burst of 7.62 mm fire. At the same instant from another support position flanking the bridge, our second machine gun opened up on the bridge and the unsuspecting guards. This enfilade of fire poured into the bodies lying around the bridge and continued for 30 seconds. Exactly 30 seconds after initiation, we "lifted and shifted" our fires, and the assault team swept over the territory, shooting any opposition and securing the far side of the position. While the assault element held the position, two specialty teams broke off and placed small amounts of explosives designed to destroy the bridge and render it useless. While the charges were being placed, the dead and wounded guerillas were searched for key documents we could exploit later. No more than three minutes after the initiation of the assault, a green star cluster flare cut through the night sky, the signal for the assault element to withdraw. We resaturated the killzone covering the withdrawal of the assaulters and continued to fire for a full minute.

Silence fell on the forest. The only noise I heard was the crackling of the cooling gun barrel as we escaped through the brush to link up with the main element at the ORP. The strike had gone well. We hit hard and were back in the brush in four minutes flat. No one said a word. No one had screamed and no orders had been shouted. The whole operation was eerily quiet. Approaching the ORP from a different route than when we left, we were challenged by the guard left behind to provide security. He let us in the small perimeter and we prepped rucks for the team to get into quickly. We had a long, heavy run through the woods that night. As the troops came into the rally point and linked up, we conducted quick checks for injuries and redistributed ammunition. All people and sensitive items were accounted for. Just before we left the perimeter, my friend Kevin leaned over grinning, "We did it! We're gonna be Green Berets!"

I couldn't let the success of the mission go to my head as we still had to evade capture and get out of the area. The mission was one of our final tests in the Special Forces qualification course. The "enemy" was a platoon of the 82nd Airborne, and they would *not* take this strike lightly. They had chased us for weeks through the mountains of central North Carolina, and I fully expected them to be on us like ugly on an ape for what we just pulled off. True to form, we spent the next six hours running through the woods and trying to keep ahead of, to the side of, or hiding from the reaction force the 82nd sent after us. These guys were good. But we were a little bit better. It's hard to describe what I felt as the sun rose on that final day and our patrol approached the phase line marking the end of training for us. I had achieved what so few in the military were able to accomplish: I was going to be a Special Forces soldier, a Green Beret.

Now, nearly thirty years later, I reflect on what has happened to our country and military since then. If you enter my office today, you will not see any awards, decorations, or degrees. The only item on display is a framed "Certificate of Training in Thumb Drive Awareness." Let me explain. In order to use military computer systems, you must first take "Thumb Drive Awareness Training" and then complete an online test. The training is informative and conveys good information—in short, it briefs well—but it takes an inordinate amount of time to complete. And here is the real kicker: thumb drives and other removable media have been banned for use in Department of Defense computers for several years!

Linked to the thumb drive awareness certificate is a requirement to complete several other classes on Information Awareness (IA). When reporting to a new unit, before you can get a user account for computers, you must undergo online computer IA training. That's right. In order to undergo the requisite IA training so that you can get a user account, you have to log on to a computer. I made the mistake once of asking, "How do you expect me to go online to get the training if I had to have the training to go online in the first place?" Looking at me like I had an appendage growing from my forehead, the IT specialist told me to "get someone else to log on and then let you use his account." After doing so and accessing the training, I received the very first lesson emphasizing the mandate to "NEVER let anyone else use your log-in or computer work station!"

The thumb drive is not a new story in the military. It is, however, a real example of the absurdity we in the military have to put up with on a daily basis and offers insight into why we are now ten years into the war on terror with no discernible objective at hand. We have created a set of rules and engagement criteria that brief well, but in order to actually identify and kill the enemy under the rules' construct, one would have to either violate the rules outright or expose oneself to administrative or even criminal sanction. One of my trusted colleagues describes the current battle climate as "Battle-Command via AR 15-6." Army Regulation 15-6, Investigations, is the policy guide for conducting administrative investigations that are often the prelude to nonjudicial or judicial punishment.

Every time a soldier fires a weapon in Iraq or Afghanistan, there is an investigation! Soldiers are constantly pulled through the wringer simply for doing what they were trained to do: kill bad guys. This investigative mindset fails to account for the inevitable second- and third-order effects of such an ill-advised rule: Soldiers fail to fire when they should; heavy weapons fail to be charged and maintained in a ready condition; and we create an environment in which soldiers who hit the ground in theater immediately begin checking off the days on their "short-time" calendars as they currently do in Korea and did in Vietnam.

We're fighting the war in yearly increments with the objective to avoid getting blown up or investigated rather than to achieve victory by vanquishing the enemy. Avoiding engagement used to be anathema to the American military warrior culture, but these days killing the enemy and celebrating the tales around the campfire at night have been replaced with a bizarre and misplaced sense that we should somehow feel guilty about such killings, complete with mandatory counseling and sensing sessions. We have created an ethos that killing our enemies is wrong, and instead of wheeling our combat formations with the single focus of victory, we are trying to figure out how to "green" the war-fighting process. Many of the stories told within the pages of this book would be outright hilarious if not for the fact that we are dealing with the deadly serious business of war, and soldiers' lives and our national survival are at stake.

Within our armed forces, we are blessed to work with dedicated, driven people. Some of the people with whom I have served in the military are brilliant. I have witnessed acts of great bravery and am regularly humbled by the hard work and dedication of our soldiers, sailors, airmen, and marines. It is for and to them that this book is written. Its purpose is to identify some correctable problems in how America prepares, decides, and goes to war.

—Jim Patterson

 I admire many of the military lawyers and judge advocates—uniformed, military attorneys serving in one of the services' Judge Advocate General's (JAG) Corps—that I have met over the years. And there is a select group of judge advocates for whom I have the highest regard: Those who have served as Command Legal Advisors for 1st Special Forces Operational Detachment—Delta (America's Delta Force). Jim Patterson is one of those judge advocates.

 I first met Jim when we were both assigned as paratroopers with America's Guard of Honor, the 82nd Airborne Division at Fort Bragg, North Carolina, in 1992. For the next two decades our paths would cross both stateside and in overseas combat zones. We share many passions—shooting, boating, and the outdoors—but none more than training soldiers, sailors, airmen, or marines in the art of killing the enemy in a manner that avoids court-martial by risk-averse commanders.

 Years of training and observing troops and commanders in conflict have led to this book. Sadly modern American military culture has bred a generation of leaders who are nothing short of risk-averse. Many fine company, battalion, and brigade commanders with whom we have had the pleasure of serving in combat in both Iraq and Afghanistan are concerned with this trend. Despite their recognition of the problem, these fine officers are often forced to remain silent. The junior troops recognize the hypocrisy but feel too stifled by rank or position to attempt to challenge it. This book is written to give voice to those warriors.

 In November 2002, I had the good fortune to be assigned as a legal advisor to Commander, Special Operations Command Central, then-Brigadier General Gary L. Harrell. Harrell—a fifteen-year veteran of the Army's Delta Force—is one of the finest warriors and commanders with whom I have had the privilege to serve. A no-nonsense straight shooter from Tennessee, Harrell has little patience for stupidity or legalese masquerading as reason. In early April 2003, I had the honor of going north into Iraq with his jump Tactical Operations Center (TOC). At his direction I briefed rules of engagement to most vanilla Special Operations Forces (SOF) in theater. Vanilla SOF are special operations forces conducting traditional special operations missions—unconventional warfare, special reconnaissance, direct action, and so on, as opposed to black SOF or National Forces units under the command and control of Joint Special Operations Command (JSOC). General Harrell's command policy on the use of force stood out in stark contrast to the policies generally articulated by his risk-averse peers in other commands. It bears quoting here:

> If any Soldier, Sailor, Airman or Marine assigned to Combined Forces Special Operations Component Command uses deadly force in self-defense they will not be judged in the clear vision of 20-20 hindsight but rather by how a reasonable person would act under situations that are tense, uncertain and rapidly evolving.

Two things I'm proud of: One is having briefed Special Forces Officer Paul Finfrock before the investigation concerning his use of deadly force in self-defense in Iraq. After the very thorough investigation, Paul told me that my briefing gave him the confidence to not hesitate and to pull the trigger when he had to kill a bad guy. It also saved him from further, unwarranted scrutiny regarding the incident.

The second thing I'm proud of is the nickname the Killing Judge given me by a SOF Sergeant Major from a Special Mission Unit. I'm proud of that name, not because it suggests a ruthless affinity with bloodshed, but because it aligns me with the soldiers who risk their lives to do what their country demands of them in battle. Many soldiers do not receive proper "top cover" from their commanders or judge advocates. It is for these soldiers that this book is written.

—David "Bo" Bolgiano

ACKNOWLEDGMENTS

Special Forces Team Sergeant, Jeff Kirkham, once remarked, "War is hard work." A seeming blinding flash of the obvious, his statement is often overlooked in the preparation for combat and, quite frankly, any important endeavor. Writing a book is hard work and without the help of the following folks, this project would have died on the vine years ago.

First, we wish to thank the good folks at Stackpole Books. The publisher, Judith Schnell, for having the faith in us from the beginning, and our patient and smart editor, Amy Lerner, for dealing with our sometimes amateurish complaints and feedback.

Next, our sincerest thanks to the folks comprising the Judgment-based Engagement Training Teams (JETs) over the past decade. We know we will miss someone out of sheer forgetfulness rather than intentionally. In no particular order: Guy "Buddy" Johnson, Jeff Rosen, Mike McKnight, John Taylor, Mark Royka, Steve Didier, Tony Lambraia, Jeff Kirkham, Nick Shoemaker, Al Goshi, Frank Short, Jim Hicks, Tom Mowell, Morgan Banks, Mark Berry, Jason "Doc" Mark, Pal Caliendo, Keith Vershay, Kyle Siegel, Doug Cox, Trish Pullar, Ethan Cole, Matt Little Sun, Fred Mabardy, George "Butch" Rogers, Frank Barile, Jeff Spears, Pavel Hr, Jose Gordon, Robert Jarman, Ray Bunn, Tim Latterner, Tom Petrowski, Tom Piddington, Chris Givvines, Geoff Wilcox, and Jeff Phillips.

The following commanders, senior leaders, and influential folks throughout the joint forces who have believed in the program and, more importantly, trusted their subordinates: Tony Parisi, Chip Swicker, Mark Kohart, Ash Naylor, Gary Harrell, Guy Walsh, Randy Watt, Steve Benden, Scott Kelly, Andy Turley, Mike Oates, Mike Steele, Brian Neal, Scott Black, Bruce Tuxill, Jim Adkins, Charlie Morgan, Charlie Dunlap, Chris Inglis, Vinny Coglianese, Frank Donovan, Dave Morris, Eldon Bargewell, Paul Finfrock, Chad McRee, Jim Helis, Jim Larsen, Tim Quillin, Jim Greer, Larry Arnold, Frank Larkin, Jim Linder, Bob Shaw, Mike Rose, Mitch Monroe, Sean Conroy, Steve Lepper, Tom Miller, Dave Bair, John Hort, Kenny Lassus, and Kevin Krause.

A special thanks to the following distinguished authors who gave freely of their time and advice: Dave Grossman, Ralph Peters, John Hall, Hays Parks, and Sean Naylor. Lastly, but most importantly, to two very special groups of people: our loved ones and all the brave warriors in the free world who truly know the cost of freedom.

INTRODUCTION

Now landsmen all, whoever you may be,
If you want to rise to the top of the tree,
If your soul isn't fettered to an office stool,
Be careful to be guided by this golden rule—
Stick close to your desks and never go to sea,
And you all may be rulers of the Queen's Navee!

From Sir Joseph—*HMS Pinafore*
(Gilbert & Sullivan, 1878)

This book is not a criticism of the hard work and sacrifice of thousands of our soldiers, sailors, airmen, and marines toiling in America's defense here and abroad. It is a critical commentary of some facets of our military's strategy. Our aim is to force some discussions—uncomfortable as they may be—in order to forge a stronger, more effective fighting force better able to protect our country.

The United States faces existential threats both internally and externally. Among the internal threats are constitutionally challenged politicians who whittle away our individual freedoms and property rights while ignoring or even undermining national security; a growing and increasingly dangerous Muslim threat manifesting itself in lone wolf actors like Major Nidal Hasan who massacred his fellow soldiers at Fort Hood; and Islamist intelligence cells—including al Qaeda—operating at mosques and universities throughout the United States. Externally our enemies are multiplying at an alarming rate, yet we systemically refuse to identify them, instead focusing on well-intentioned but unwinnable efforts at nation-building and self-inflicted counterinsurgency operations. Shifts in military goals, allocation of the resources in America's discretionary budget, and self-imposed legal restrictions have reduced America's ability and capacity to wage war and, consequently, guarantee her security. Moreover, such shifts threaten the social contract between the republic and her citizen soldiers. While misinterpretations of law and policy—both ignorant and willful—have engendered this trend, opportunities do exist to restore the strength and proper role of the armed forces of the United States. With over fifty years of combined military, legal, and law enforcement experience, we will address and discuss these issues through the lenses of what we know best: the law and the military.

Adherence to the rule of law in combat often requires the United States to fight with one hand tied behind its back even when our enemies may not be so inhibited, yet this is the price we have historically paid, and must continue to pay, in order to maintain the moral high ground and uphold our national principles. Recent developments in policy and revisionist interpretations of the law of armed conflict now dangerously handicap America by forcing her to fight shackled with unjustifiable restrictions born of misguided globalism. This behavior is both corrosive and dangerous. At an institutional level such a course of action risks violating the social contract between our government and its citizen soldiers. At the individual level, it unnecessarily jeopardizes the lives of our warriors. A soldier's duty, like that of a police officer, is perilous enough without having anonymous bureaucrats in Washington trying to direct and fine-tune tactics with a ten-thousand-mile screwdriver.

As a nation we have become confused not only about the true nature of our national interests, but also about choosing the appropriate instrument of power to reach those objectives. An apt illustration of this confusion is the following commentary concerning military intelligence collection methods in Afghanistan, authored by Major General Michael T. Flynn while Deputy Chief of Staff, Intelligence (CJ2) for the International Security Assistance Force in Afghanistan, Captain Matt Pottinger, USMC, and Paul D. Batchelor, DIA:

> The highly complex environment in Afghanistan requires an adaptive way of thinking and operating. *Just as the old rules of warfare may no longer apply,* a new way of leveraging and applying the information spectrum requires substantive improvements. The ISAF Joint Command (IJC) under the leadership of Lieutenant General David M. Rodriguez has made some recent innovative strides with the advent of the "Information Dominance Center." This type of innovation must be mirrored to the degree possible at

multiple levels of command and back in our intelligence community structures in the United States. In no way is this a perfect solution and the United States will continue to adapt. However, the United States must constantly change our way of operating and thinking if we want to win.[1] [emphasis added]

General Flynn assumes, as do most senior leaders, that the old rules of warfare no longer apply. This assumption is not being sufficiently challenged by our civilian and military leaders, who seem content to fritter away billions of dollars and the lives of America's warriors in a counterinsurgency fight with no apparent end or achievable goal. General Flynn's last sentence, although probably not for the reasons intended, is exactly right. Our national interest has not been clearly defined in Afghanistan. Moreover, if the enemy and environment remains "human terrain," then the military is probably not the right element of our national power to achieve lasting, meaningful success. Unless we intend to annihilate major civilian populations in that unstable, primarily Muslim region of the world, the continued American military presence is arguably a waste of our national resources. The Department of State, USAID, or the Peace Corps could more appropriately address the challenges as General Flynn articulates them than could our armed services. Unfortunately, in the military, our leadership and strategic thinkers do not recognize this and continue to hammer away at fighting the counterinsurgency fight and morphing the military from a warfighting entity into a diplomatic corps focused on nation-building.

The military relies, in part, on its system of schools to develop mental agility, creativity, and innovative thinking in its leaders. These schools—the services' Command and General Staff and War Colleges—aspire to promote critical thinking and honest appraisal of the warfighting art. Too often, however, the curriculum relies on concepts fed from above: Counterinsurgency (COIN); Interagency/Whole of Government; and, panoplies of New Age Globalism. Warriors who truly challenge or question such concepts are quickly marginalized. This is most evident in our analysis of current conflicts in the Muslim world. Instead of questioning the efficacy or propriety of using the military to achieve America's goals, or even questioning the propriety of such goals, most students simply accept as fact that COIN is the way ahead.

The study of Thucydides is a staple for military officers attending the services' war colleges, yet the lessons learned are often overlooked by senior military and political strategists. Take for instance the lessons learned from the Sicilian expedition, the Athenian attempt to conquer Sicily from 415 to 413 B.C. during an interlude to the Peloponnesian Wars. The tactical commanders at the front routinely reported the foolhardiness of attempting to conquer the island. The Athenian general, Nicias, ignored the tactical realities and instead militated for his own version of a surge, falsely assuming that all the Athenians needed to win was more troops. While his efforts proved successful in the short run—he won the battle—the effort eventually led to the splintering and disintegration of the republic. The Athenians desperately needed an alternate course of action, yet succumbed to the direction of the general.

An alternative view to COIN and nation-building today might hold that the only interaction with certain regions of the world, especially countries ruled under some form of Sharia law, should be on an economic and trade basis. This would include most of the Maghreb, the Arabian Peninsula, Iran, Pakistan, and Afghanistan. Militarily we should be prepared to return as necessary to obliterate al Qaeda—and that should continue so long as it remains a threat to us in the West—but the military is ill-suited legally and operationally to effect social change to the degree promised or envisioned by both presidents Bush and Obama. Sharia-compliant populations do not want a constitutional democratic form of government, and our attempts to force the matter are, not surprisingly, seen as unwelcome attempts at imperialism. Moreover, such attempts invite a violent response, sometimes involving airplanes being flown into buildings.

In other words, "the old rules of military force no longer apply" *only* if we continue to fall into the trap of entering into forays unnecessarily and then compound the error by playing by our opponents' rules. We choose to go down a road we did not need to take, jump into a manhole with both feet, and suddenly wonder why we are in such a predicament. Yet no one at our senior levels of leadership dares to voice such an opinion publicly or officially, mostly out of fear of missing the next assignment or promotion.

Such folly is felt most acutely at the tactical level. Yes, the military mission is often perilous. It often falls to the commander to rally his troops to "seize the hill" or "attack that position." But it is criminally negligent to order troops to seize the hill with pitchforks when machine guns are readily available. Sadly that is what the United States is doing to its warriors on a daily basis by misinterpreting and misapplying the Law of War and the rules of engagement.

CHAPTER ONE

The Shift from Killing the Enemy to Nation-Building

A dramatic but unnoticed shift in foreign policy began to emerge early in the Clinton administration. Mirroring the thinking of Woodrow Wilson, Clinton's National Security Advisor Anthony Lake and Secretary of State Madeleine Albright pushed an agenda that essentially stated that the United States could disregard sovereign territorial boundaries to promote humanitarian goals. This was in stark contrast to the realpolitik of Henry Kissinger, who famously opened doors with China while ignoring that nation's internal oppressions, and Ronald Reagan's Weinberger Doctrine of limited goals and clearly defined end states, a strategy exemplified by Operation Desert Storm, the rollback of Iraq's invasion of Kuwait during the administration of President George H. W. Bush. These common sense notions are pithily summarized by General Howell Estes in a *Frontline* interview:

> It's really as simple as this. . . . You don't commit militaries unless there's a vital interest to the nation at risk. You don't commit militaries unless you are going to commit a decisive force. You give them clear objectives, you have a defined exit strategy, so you know what gets you in and what gets you out. And you let the military do what they're designed to do.[2]

The shifts in the Clinton administration's policy toward using the military for nation-building and stability operations rather than war led to

America's ill-fated missions in Somalia, Haiti, Bosnia, and Kosovo. Kosovo, while invigorating the new Effects-based Operations (EBO) so highly touted by those enamored of the so-called Revolution of Military Affairs, completely ignored the second- and third-order effects such an operation had on the West's position vis-à-vis the Muslim world and Russia. The perceived hypocrisy of such lofty-sounding goals was much in evidence when America ignored the true failed-state-induced genocides occurring in Rwanda and later in Darfur. This policy is now so deeply entrenched in the thinking of those crafting military and national security strategies that they now can't or won't define our enemies or clarify our strategic goals even after September 11.

Many of those now making strategic policy view the world through a postmodern lens of idealism. They believe in the subordination of national interest to globalism, and they are simply unaware of the Hobbesian lens through which our enemies see us. If an idealist enters a forum with a realist and ignores the rules by which the realist operates, the realist will eat the idealist for lunch. Henry Kissinger understood this perfectly when he stated, "While we should never give up our principles, we must also realize that we cannot maintain our principles unless we survive." The idealists who currently occupy our seats of power do not realize this. For too many years, no one in Washington has shown an understanding of what war and the coercive use of military power represents. War is "the use of sustained organized violence by an actor against an adversary with the intent to achieve the actor's policy objectives in relation to the system."[3]

After the direct attacks of September 11, America rightly and justly used military force—war—to enter Afghanistan with the clearly defined military mission of killing or capturing members of al Qaeda and destroying their training camps. Our invasion and attack were preceded by a warning, affording the Taliban an opportunity to produce the al Qaeda operatives and shut down their training camps. How such a righteous, specific, and achievable goal could dissolve into the ahistoric pipedream of the nation-building mission of developing a democratically elected nation-state out of thirty-seven distinct tribal communities is mind-boggling. And yet the nation-building mission creep began right after the Battle of Tora Bora and has grown in size and scope ever since. As we used to say as young paratroopers in the 82nd Airborne Division when an absurd mission came down from higher headquarters: "Just strap that ballistic helmet on tight and bash your head into the wall three times and it will begin to make sense!"

In purely fiscal terms, America's war efforts in Afghanistan, Iraq, and Libya have been a disaster in these hard economic times. A report out of Brown University estimates that the U.S. wars will cost $4 trillion and leave 225,000 dead, including both civilians and soldiers. Even the conservative Congressional Budget Office has placed a $1.8 trillion federal price tag on the wars.[4] To what end? Afghanistan is still a corruption-plagued feudal backwater. Iraq is a little better off, but for how long after we pull out? The jury is still out on Libya and the rest of the crowd—Yemen, Pakistan, and Somalia—as we continue to pour blood and treasure after these bad investments with no explanation as to how they positively affect our national interest.

Paraphrasing Dag Hammarskjöld, many military leaders now repeat the mantra that the military is the only element of power with the *capacity* to do these missions. But then we, America in general and her military specifically, are stuck with doing it. Moreover, this approach only encourages our involvement in other contingencies, benefitting no one save defense contractors who reap huge paydays and senior military officers seeking promotion.

The Country witnessed this folly in World War II when America wasted money on the Burma-China Road and airfields in China. Commenting on America's propensity to embark upon such shortsighted ventures, Winston Churchill observed:

> On both counts therefore we argued that the enormous expenditure of manpower and material would not be worthwhile. But we never succeeded in deflecting the Americans from their purpose. Their national psychology is such that the bigger the Idea the more wholeheartedly and obstinately do they throw themselves into making it a success. It is an admirable characteristic, provided the *Idea* is good.[5]

The problem today is that no one within the civilian or military leadership is seriously questioning the *idea* of Afghanistan, and therefore the warrior on the ground is left holding the bag.

Once the military accepts a mission—no matter how absurd or illfocused—its culture is to carry it out as best able. This concept is aptly illustrated by General Petreaus's account of meeting with President Obama and being appointed to take over Afghanistan. Petreaus quipped: "When the President asks you to do something, the only answer is 'yes.'"

General officer after general officer appear on the stages of our war colleges repeating phrases such as "Just because it is hard does not mean it can't be done" or "Just because Alexander the Great, the British, and the Russians failed to conquer and control Afghanistan, does not mean that we can't do it." Ignoring Clausewitz's sage guidance that "policy is not a tyrant, that is, it cannot demand of strategy that which it cannot deliver," many smart and well-intentioned people enter the policy debate and influence the planning and execution of military strategy operating on the flawed and unexamined premises we are attempting to shed light on in this book. Thousands upon thousands of hours are spent needlessly and futilely tilling the same tired ground: how to win the COIN fight. Ignoring the history and culture of the region, with an occasional bow to the tribal leaders, America vainly believes that if we can just figure out "the systems and the metrics," we can win.

In an attempt to make strategy from ill-advised policy, such smart people create monstrosities like former Commander of the International Security Assistance Force (ISAF) General Stanley McChrystal's infamous spaghetti diagram, purporting to show the factors to consider in forging a path to success in the counterinsurgency fight in Afghanistan. While McChrystal was ignominiously sacked by Barack Obama in June 2010, his successors showed little inclination of straying from the COIN mantra.

Such complexity is too difficult to manage and implement even here in the United States. To try to impose such Western-based solutions on a Third World country like Afghanistan that lacks infrastructure, literacy, and a like-minded culture is the height of arrogance and absurdity. ISAF Headquarters (the troops now derisively call ISAF "I Saw Americans Fighting" due to the noncombative nature of our "allies") talks a good game of putting an Afghan face on plans and operations, but you really have to question how much Afghan influence there is on the policy decisions being made. From the reintegration of the Taliban to poppy eradication, NATO and other foreign influences are involved down to the last detail. Everyone toils away putting in eighteen-hour days churning out plan after plan to what end? At the senior policy level, no one asks the magic question, "How does this further America's national interest?" Consequently, at the operational level, no one asks, "What are our achievable objectives?"

Afghanistan Stability / COIN Dynamics

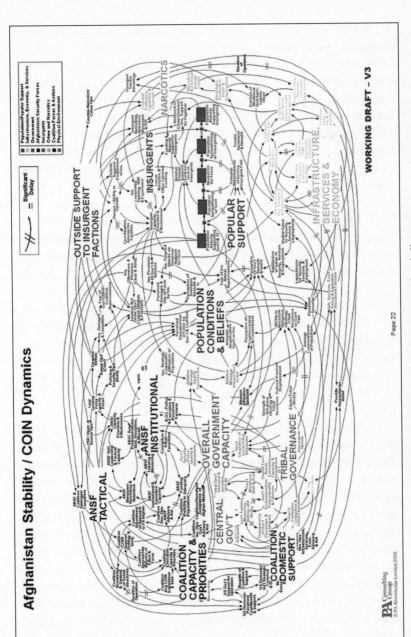

Stan McChrystal's infamous spaghetti diagram.

WORKING DRAFT – V3

This is what happens when America lacks a clearly defined grand strategy. We were in the second year of the Obama administration without a published National Security Strategy (NSS), but of course the problem predates Barack Obama: he is merely the latest caretaker or steward of Gondor from Tolkien's *The Lord of the Rings*. We desperately need an Aragorn, a true leader.

To paraphrase the Cheshire Cat from *Alice in Wonderland*, "If you don't know where you are going, any road will get you there!" The Carnegie Endowment for International Peace sees the folly of our course in Afghanistan:

> The current strategy, which is based on expecting quick results, especially with regard to the Afghan National Army, is unrealistic and self-defeating. It is simply not feasible to transform a (mostly illiterate) force of 60,000 into a well-functioning army of 250,000 in only a few years, regardless of outside assistance. Afghanization—enabling Afghans to take primary responsibility for their security—could potentially take a decade. Lower casualties should be a recognized objective of a new strategy, and the debate should be more about the assessment of the current strategy than about troop numbers. The United States must reallocate its limited resources to correspond with its interests.[6]

Nevertheless, American military leaders, without clear guidance from their civilian masters, continue to flounder in Afghanistan at a tremendous cost in American treasure and blood. Their battalion- and brigade-level commanders toil ever harder, attempting to negotiate the tightrope between force protection and the COIN doctrine. Astoundingly, Generals today act on the premise that "an atrocity is not necessarily what one actually does, but what one is successfully blamed for."[7] A clandestine operative immersed in our current operations conducted behind the scenes in Afghanistan sums it up: "Of course our policy is failing. How else could America enter into a country of warriors and in eight years fail to raise an army?" The reality may be that we are fighting an insurgency rather than a counterinsurgency and just don't know it.[8]

From Haiti, Somalia, and Kosovo in the nineties, to Iraq and Afghanistan in the ongoing war on terror, the United States has misused its armed forces in a misguided attempt to spread democracy rather than hunt and kill its enemies. In the January 2010 edition of *Joint Force Quarterly*, we find the following perspective on how to achieve success in Afghanistan: "[Success] requires proper resourcing, effective governance, incorporation of traditional village and district *shuras*, public access to social services, an end to corruption, and local dispute resolution mechanisms." Then the author adds the obligatory, "This will not be easy. But difficult is not impossible."[9] Really? At what cost and to what end?

Such efforts have eroded the military's ability to confront true existential global threats, those in which the scope and intensity are so high they negatively affect the population as a whole, such as nuclear events or economic collapse. Admiral Mike Mullen, Chairman of the Joint Chiefs of Staff, comments, "In providing my best military advice of the past two years, I have emphasized that military activities must support rather than lead foreign policy."[10]

What Mike Mullen should more forcefully state is that the operationally focused COIN doctrine, while it has its place, should not become America's grand strategy. But sadly it has become just that. Michael J. Mazarr makes a cogent point in *The Washington Quarterly*:

> The rapidly emerging conventional wisdom in U.S. defense policy suggests that the dominant threats we face today and will face over the coming decades are nontraditional, asymmetrical, and insurgent-terrorist in character, rather than the large-scale, interstate war about which U.S. defense planners obsessed from the 1930s until about 1989. . . . This conventional wisdom builds on thoughtful concepts of the future of warfare and has the best interests of the United States very much at heart but, if taken seriously, would distort U.S. defense priorities for years to come and trap the U.S. armed forces in endless conflicts that military power cannot win."[11]

As we shall see, the expansion of COIN doctrine into a grand strategy also has the negative effect of diminishing our forces' military effectiveness—killing power—and even our notions of self-preservation. Minimum force may be a perfectly appropriate strategic concept in the COIN fight (i.e., one may not wish to drop a 2,000-pound JDAM bomb on a village), but it is horrible tactical guidance for a soldier on the ground using force in response to an imminent threat of death or serious bodily injury. Moreover, it is anathema to a military's ability to conduct violent, force-on-force combat operations. Yet due to a deadly combination of misinformed legal oversight and risk-averse command climate, that is exactly what is happening time and again in our current theaters of war.

Some are determined to expand such behavior beyond our current efforts in Afghanistan. In an effort to better define our war on terror some, such as Daniel G. Cox, writing in the *Joint Force Quarterly*, argue that failed states and ungoverned spaces become breeding grounds for al Qaeda and therefore kinetic options—that is, killing bad guys—will not ultimately be successful:

> Successfully countering al Qaeda in Iraq and Afghanistan, while vital, does not necessarily encompass all that needs to be done to counter a global insurgency. Unfortunately, the old counterinsurgency mantra "clear, hold, build" now applies to almost everywhere there is an exploitable instability. Kinetic options will likely meet with limited success as the main course of action, as the al Qaeda movement has spread deeply into multiple states and regions, and no coalition force could hope to intervene militarily in all of these places simultaneously . . . Stability operations performed by the military take on prime importance in such a struggle.[12]

While pure kinetic operations, or "stamping on fleas," may not be totally effective in the COIN environment, they certainly maintain their primary importance in general warfare. Arguing that the United States needs to be more and more involved in stability operations ignores what should be the prime question: How does our involvement in stability operations in "Country X" accrue to our national interest? Such an approach could bankrupt the treasuries of the West in short order. Moreover, the mere presence of Western troops in multiple Islamic countries may very well add tinder to the fires of radicalism. If undertaken, nation-building and stability operations should be handled by elements of power other than our military. If we don't have them, we need to develop them—if we decide it to be in our best interest to nation-build.

In response to criticism and questioning of our policies, globalists point to the success of the Marshall Plan implemented in Germany and

Western Europe after World War II. Such an analogy to today doesn't hold. First, we totally defeated Nazi Germany, and the large majority of American people did not question the necessity of going to war. In 1945, there was no doubt among the population of Germany about who was in charge. Moreover, the alternative—being absorbed into Stalin's Soviet sphere—was not a popular option for the German people. Fear is a tremendous motivator. Lastly, despite the tremendous differences between the German Nazi state and our constitutional, republican form of government, the social differences between the German people and their conquerors were minimal. Germany was a strongly Evangelical Protestant and Roman Catholic country. National Socialism was a convenient detour in their escape from the double miseries of the Great Depression and the manacles of the Versailles Treaty imposed after the First World War.

In Iraq, however, the United States did not totally defeat the population. Such a war of annihilation was not our intent from the outset, nor should it have been. The same holds true in Afghanistan. In April 2004, during the first Battle of Fallujah, a foreign Special Forces commander claimed that the quickest way for the United States to win in Fallujah and defeat the insurgency in Iraq would be for America to level Fallujah with a B-52 strike while Al Jazeera film crews broadcast the destruction. Instead, going to the opposite extreme, America hamstrung its marines with absurd ROE (Rules of Engagement) constructs that did not even allow marine snipers to target enemy military-age males carrying AK-47s scurrying from building to building.

Even if coalition forces had overwhelmingly defeated the Iraqi or Afghan populations, the West has ignored the fact that they are a different breed of people. A veneer of globalism, conflated by the Internet, leads many to overlook this fact. While they may have a McDonald's in town, they hold substantively different values than we do. We are often fooled by the feel-good smiles we receive after handing out medicine and food, building schools, and all the other nation-building efforts we are involved in. The population will revert to its roots. Those roots, especially in Afghanistan, are not pro-Western or democratic. It would take a cataclysmic event or a complete subjugation of their populaces to turn them into anything remotely resembling a democracy. Ignoring these truths, America, led by our military, continues to follow courses of action that fritter away our warriors' lives and drain our treasuries.

CHAPTER TWO

First, Identify the Enemy

A combination of political correctness gone astray and the diminution of what should be a declaration of war to the criminal law arena has prevented the United States and the West from clearly identifying the enemy. The enemy is a militarized, globalized Islamic jihad that does not suffer from an identity crisis. Yet America persists in treating this Islamist threat with soft power and the enemy combatants as criminals, as evidenced by the Christmas 2009 bomber incident where the FBI read a non-U.S. person his rights after he attempted to blow up an airliner during its approach to Detroit Metro Airport. This strategy is doomed to failure and actually creates more jihadist enemies. According to Michael Scheuer, "The Muslim worlds . . . grew slowly resistant and then directly hostile to American soft power, seeing its attributes as something not to aspire to but to ward off for reasons of faith or national identity or both."[13]

Former Director of the Central Intelligence Agency Michael Hayden spoke directly and forcefully in a January 3, 2010, *Washington Post* op-ed:

> We got it wrong in Detroit on Christmas Day. We allowed an enemy combatant the protections of our Constitution before we had adequately interrogated him. Umar Farouk Abdulmutallab is not "an isolated extremist." He is the tip of the spear of a complex al-Qaeda plot to kill Americans in our homeland.[14]

Senior military leaders within the Department of Defense have turned their backs on what ought to be obvious. Former Deputy Secretary of Defense Gordon England dismissed one clarion of truth in the Pentagon: Army Major Stephen Coughlin, who had the guts to call this spade a spade. Gordon England's political sensitivity and belief in globalism did not allow room for the possibility that even if only a small percentage of the world's Muslim population were true jihadists, they would still represent an existential threat to America. This blind obeisance to political correctness is frighteningly dangerous. Quoting from Major Coughlin's unclassified thesis submitted in fulfillment of his masters of strategic intelligence degree from the National Defense Intelligence College:

> Just as we ignored *Mein Kampf* "to our great detriment" prior to World War II, so we are on the verge of suffering a similar fate today. The reason the Intelligence Community is unable to define the nature of the *jihadi* enemy . . . is because we have not "read what the enemy has said." In other words, we have failed to undertake an assessment of the threat based on the *jihadi* enemy's declared strategic doctrine.[15]

Coughlin clearly identifies not only the blindness of our political leaders but more disturbingly the willful gross negligence of our intelligence communities that ignore the Islamic threat due to political correctness:

> Do we really know, as the President asserts, that the "terrorists are traitors to their own faith"? Even if they are, are they not traitors in the context of an Islamic belief structure that fuels "extremist" doctrine? While certainly not his intent, the President's statements holding Islam harmless continue to have a chilling effect on the unconstrained threat analysis of an enemy that openly declares that they fight *jihad* in furtherance of Islamic causes—regardless of whether those causes are ultimately properly aligned with Islam.[16]

Whether Coughlin overstates the threat is open to debate, but when he was scheduled to appear as a guest lecturer at a senior service school in 2009, he was unceremoniously disinvited at the last minute because his comments might offend some of the Muslim students. So much for encouraging open, critical thinking skills that are supposedly the hallmark of our senior service schools. "Islam is a religion of peace" might be a fine strategic communications bullet, but is it an honest reference point for accurate intelligence analysis and policy debate? This claim needs to be put to rigorous analysis.

Coughlin was asked to research and validate the extent to which Islam is fueling radicalism and producing such virulent actors. Coughlin's research led him to the same conclusion as other scholars: It is not a few "radicalized" (the current socially acceptable and focus-group tested term) jihadists being led astray—it is Islam itself. Islam was and is spread by the sword, not by any benign sense of universal or existential good. Coughlin had the intellectual rigor and courage to discover that the Quran means exactly what it says. Furthermore, he raised the clarion call that we are grossly negligent in not adjusting our doctrine and strategy to address this threat. For his efforts, he was summarily dismissed, and several articles disparaging him were published. Steve Coughlin challenged the mantra that "Islam is a religion of peace." Identifying one's adversary should be the first step in devising a responsible and adequate defense.

Perhaps identifying an enemy goes against the mindset of strategic leaders and educators who hold that everything we face is within the context of a volatile, uncertain, complex, and ambiguous (VUCA) environment. VUCA has been repeated so often that it has become nearly self-fulfilling.

The etiology of VUCA may be found in Sun Tzu's writings. "Much strategy prevails over little strategy, so those with no strategy cannot but be defeated. Therefore it is said that victorious warriors win first and then go to war, while defeated warriors go to war first and then seek to win."[17]

Sun Tzu's quote makes sense when read as admonition against ineffectual planning, but it creates chaos when read as a strategic blueprint mandating complexity. When taken to its logical extreme, Sun Tzu's guidance implies that all "important" issues must be complex. If read literally—as it appears to have been by many strategic thinkers—a simple solution to an important problem could never be the right answer. This heels-over-head approach causes many otherwise sound policies to be ignored simply because they do not meet the complexity standard of the VUCAphiles. It also violates the rule of Occam's razor.

Occam's razor is the principle that entities must not be multiplied beyond necessity, and the simplest explanation or strategy tends to be the best one. We have tended to jump right over one simple rule: Do not use the military except when you intend to use overwhelming force to quell an important, if not existential, threat. It was appropriate to deploy American military forces to Afghanistan in 2001 to kill al Qaeda and its henchmen. It was inviting a VUCA environment to stay in that country pursuing imprecise, often shifting goals not of a pure military nature. Just like Brer Rabbit got stuck after punching the figure his nemeses made of tar, Afghanistan is the United States' tar baby, and we're getting more and more entangled in the mire. To date, no senior civilian or military leader has clearly articulated the vital strategic interest at stake to require that the United States military remain in Afghanistan.

Osama bin Laden never hid his goals: restoration of an Islamic caliphate in the traditional Muslim lands and the *eventual* destruction of the West.

The ruling to kill the Americans and their allies—civilians and military—is an individual duty for every Muslim who can do it in any country in which it is possible to do it, in order to liberate the al-Aqsa Mosque and the holy mosque from their grip, and in order for their armies to move out of all the lands of Islam, defeated and unable to threaten any Muslim.[18]

Inhabitants of high-rise apartment buildings in the Bailey's Crossroads section of northern Virginia broke into frenzied celebration after the September 11 attacks and hundreds of mosques here in the United States are being used as Islamic intelligence centers—these should be clues.[19] When Army Major Nidal Hasan committed an overt act of terror at Fort Hood, the VUCAphiles attributed it to everything but the obvious. Instead of recognizing Hasan as the tip of an enemy-within iceberg, they searched for other explanations, no matter how far-fetched: "He was suffering from post-traumatic stress disorder once removed" or "He was just a strange, lonely young man whose seeking of fulfillment was manifested in violence." Charles Krauthammer summarizes:

What a surprise—that someone who shouts "Allahu Akbar" (the "God is great" jihadist battle cry) as he is shooting up a room of

American soldiers might have Islamist motives. It certainly was a surprise to the mainstream media, which spent the weekend after the Fort Hood massacre downplaying Nidal Hasan's religious beliefs.[20]

Further heaping pain upon the families of the murdered victims were the comments by the Army's Chief of Staff General George Casey. Casey, a casualty of the risk-averse pandemic among his generation of general officers, stood firmly in his politically correct but out of touch DoD world when he stated that "the loss of diversity in the army would have been a bigger tragedy" than the loss of lives. The thought of manning up and telling the truth to the families of the slain soldiers instead of parroting back the talking points he has been fed throughout his career probably never crossed his mind. And this is the man that—after demonstrating a mediocre performance as top commander in Iraq—the army promoted to Chief of Staff. It should not come as a surprise, however, as Casey was one of many of Wesley Clark's progenies from the Balkans, where risk-averse leadership was the norm. It was in the Balkans where the military began to reward soldiers for not using force.

When the Department of Defense undertook a review of the Fort Hood shootings, they looked everywhere but the obvious for the cause of such an attack. The report, coauthored by Admiral Vern Clark and Togo West Jr., focused on what signals were missed, mistakes made by Hasan's supervisors, and how such an incident could be avoided in the future.

One should have expected that such a fix was in when West, a former Army JAG and Secretary of the Army under Clinton, and Clark, a former Chief of Naval Operations, were appointed. Both arguably had an interest to protect because in the 1990s they were responsible for foisting the very same politically correct and broken system that is in place today. Then leaders such as West implemented COO (consideration of others) programs. COO training was vaulted to the top of the training calendar as a means of showing to the casual observer just how seriously the military took diversity. Firing ranges, parachute jumping, and physical fitness all took a backseat to COO training. Even today we are left with mandatory EO (equal opportunity) training and sexual assault prevention training because senior leaders just don't trust their subordinates.

When releasing the Fort Hood report on January 15, 2010, the investigators never mentioned Islamic extremists or Hasan by name. Instead, they bent over backward in cautioning against thinking that the threat stems only from Islamic fundamentalism. The report—complete with an obligatory white-hand-gripping-black-hand photo on the cover—is a perfect combination of whitewash and overreaction. It focuses on trying to perceive which individuals are at risk for violent behavior rather than looking at the threat posed by Islamic groups.[21] Moreover, it focuses on the effects of post-traumatic stress disorder: something totally unconnected to the events at Fort Hood except in the twisted clouds of Nidal Hasan's criminal defense team's strategic communication effort launched almost immediately post-incident.

Quoting from the Clark-West report: "The range of contributing factors for different types of violence is diverse. Although some factors, such as low self-esteem, depression, and anger are tied to many different types of violence, others are more particular to specific types of aggression. Any form of extremism—whether it is grounded in racist or religious ideology—remains of equal concern to the Department of Defense." Using near-Orwellian language in its effort to appear nondiscriminatory, the report ignores that Nidal Hasan is an Islamic extremist—an enemy within—who acted in compliance with the dictates of Sharia law. Instead it searches for all other possible reasons no matter how absurd or tangential, treating these incidents just like any other incident of workplace violence.

The military has begun eating its own by now disciplining at least eight officers for failing to take action against Hasan. These former army supervisors were no doubt afraid to discipline him because of rampant political correctness. They believed, and rightly so, that if they took action against Hasan when he handed out business cards that said "Soldier of Allah" or reprimanded him for preaching anti-war Islam to wounded warriors, they themselves would be investigated and disciplined for not showing tolerance or ignoring the spirit of inclusiveness mandated by Equal Opportunity (EO), the remnants of Wesley Clark and Togo West's COO program.

The Fort Hood report failed to examine the victims' inability to exercise their inherent right of self-defense. The military prohibits anyone from carrying sidearms: anyone except the DoD police, and they were minutes away from responding to a threat that demanded instantaneous response. Unbelievably, the report underscores how the government should control its soldiers' private ownership of firearms.[22] Thirteen brave Americans died and forty-three others were wounded because of this dereliction, but it was never even addressed. More later on this perfidy, but all you really need to remember is that guns cause crime like spoons cause Rosie O'Donnell to be fat. And spoons can't stop a killer like Hasan. Despite this blinding flash of the obvious, here is one of the Department of Defense's responses:

> The Pentagon will adopt a broad policy governing how privately owned guns can be carried or stored at military installations following the shooting deaths of 13 people last year at Fort Hood, Texas.
>
> A disgruntled Army doctor is charged in the deaths.
>
> Maj. Nidal Hasan had little or no access to military firearms in his job as a psychologist, but was able to buy two handguns and bring them onto the base.[23]

The military will continue to restrict the ability of its soldiers to exercise their inherent right of self-defense by ensuring they are disarmed. And calling Nidal Hasan "a disgruntled Army doctor" instead of a fanatical Muslim is akin to calling Adolf Hitler "a disgruntled former army corporal." The absurdity and dangerousness of the Army's tepid response has recently been underscored by another plot to attack soldiers at a military personnel center.

Two men have been charged in a suicide terror plot aimed at a Seattle federal building used to induct new recruits into the armed services. Abu Khalid Abdul-Latif and Walli Mujahidh, incensed about American military activities in Afghanistan, Iraq, and Yemen, believed that jihad in America should be a physical jihad and not just media jihad, that they should take action rather than just talk. Specifically referring to the 2009 Fort Hood massacre, Abdul-Latif further declared that if one person could kill so many people, three attackers could kill many more.[24]

The enemy has become adept at utilizing lawfare against us. Major General Charles J. Dunlap Jr. explained lawfare as "the strategy of using— or misusing—law as a substitute for traditional military means to achieve an operational objective."[25] Instead of recognizing and countering it, we have—with the able assistance of the supporting lawyers in the ACLU, our Federal Judiciary, and even the Department of Justice—buried our collective heads in the sand.

On November 20, 2006, Federal Air Marshals removed six Muslim imams from US Airways Flight 300 in Minneapolis, Minnesota, after several passengers and crew members witnessed the imams displaying extremely suspicious behavior. Passengers reported the men had been praying loudly in the terminal, chanting "Allah, Allah" and cursing U.S. policies in Iraq. Once on board, the men took tactically positioned seats allowing them positions of dominance in the cabin's front, middle, and back. Two imams, while not overweight, asked for seat belt extenders with heavy metal buckles that could be used as weapons. The pilot was told that three of the men had one-way tickets. A passenger who spoke Arabic said one imam expressed fundamentalist views. At best, the imams' actions appeared to be intentionally provocative in the aftermath of September 11. The airport police and Federal Air Marshal agreed the circumstances were suspicious enough to warrant asking the men to leave the airplane. The captain delayed takeoff and had the imams removed, and the plane left without the imams on board about three hours later. The imams were detained, questioned, and eventually released.

All of the above seems like rather prudent and rational conduct on behalf of the authorities. The imams, however, along with the Muslim American Society and the Council on American-Islamic Relations, filed suit against the airline, saying they were removed from the airplane solely due to religious discrimination. On July 24, 2009, U.S. District Judge Ann Montgomery allowed the discrimination lawsuit filed by the imams to proceed, remarking, "The right not to be arrested in the absence of probable cause is clearly established and, based on the allegations . . . no reasonable officer could have believed that the arrest of the Plaintiffs was proper." You could safely argue that no reasonable officer would *not* have detained the imams under such circumstances. Yet now, even after the Christmas Day 2009 attempted bombing by a Nigerian-born Islamic jihadist, Transportation Security Agency (TSA) personnel are still busily strip-searching octogenarian American grandmothers. We don't want to be accused of profiling. Islamists 1: America 0 in this round of lawfare.

Another example of how radical Islam uses lawfare against the West comes out of Amsterdam. There, in January 2010, Dutch prosecutors began their criminal trial against Geert Wilders. His crime: offending the Netherland's Muslim minority by comparing the Quran to Hitler's *Mein Kampf* and calling for it to be banned in the Netherlands. Wilders also produced the 2008 short film *Fitna*, which offended Muslims around the world by juxtaposing Quranic verses with images of terrorism by Islamic radicals. The Muslim minority is of course free to riot and cause mayhem if a Danish cartoonist draws another Mohammed "Bombhead" cartoon. Moreover, most publishers here and in Europe will not publish the cartoon out of fear of Islamic reprisal and a self-imposed political correctness.

On the active counter-terror front, if our national intelligence pin-points a suspected member of al Qaeda in Afghanistan or Pakistan we do not hesitate (nor should we) in launching a hellfire missile in an armed Predator strike on that target. But if that same al Qaeda member is run-ning an intelligence center out of a mosque in Minneapolis, the policy makers at DOJ wring their hands over whether or not we can listen in on his telephone conversations! Under the provisions of the Foreign Intelli-gence Surveillance Act (FISA), FBI agents need a court order and proba-ble cause to listen in on non-U.S. person Islamic extremists' phone conversations. Incredibly, there are fifth columnists currently sitting on both sides of the aisle who willingly advocate against the reduction of even the slightest of protections with regard to FISA. Hard to imagine that Franklin Delano Roosevelt had German spies shot and hung, either when they were caught in the act or after they were detained and tried by military tribunal.

Today we spend hundreds of millions of dollars arguing over whether or not unlawful combatants can be tried by military tribunals, and then we self-flagellate over our alleged maltreatment of individuals whose hearts and souls are dedicated to our destruction. Our Justice Department interro-gates not terrorists but CIA employees for abuses they allegedly commit when questioning real terrorists!

Treating unlawful enemy combatants as mere criminal defendants to be prosecuted and not enemies to be killed is wrong from both a legal and a policy perspective. It confers a protected status upon brigands never envisaged by civilized nations, except in most recent times. This trend, amplified by the Obama administration, plays right into the hands of our enemies.

The rising tide of Islam and its intrusion in the West and modernity needs to be addressed. According to Samuel Helfont of Princeton Univer-sity's Department of Near Eastern Studies:

Comprehending this relationship is vital for appreciating how an increasing number of Muslims understand and practice their religion in a rapidly changing world. This dynamic is also essential for policymakers because it forms the foundation of modern Islamist political thought, which has become increasingly popular throughout Middle East.[26]

America should, in the near term, refrain from interfering in the internal policy mechanisms of Islamic states, instead respecting their sovereignty and self-determination. And on the other hand, America should signal clearly to those same nations, and to the Islamic world as a whole, that we will not tolerate the institutionalization of Sharia law in our constitutional republic. Take the concept of *dhimmi,* which refers to a non-Muslim subject of a state governed in accordance with Sharia law, usually in a state of servitude. We may be *dhimmi* in your country, but not here. In fact, if you want to immigrate to America or practice your religion here, you must learn to render unto Caesar what is Caesar's and not attempt to bring Sharia here. In essence, you can freely practice your religion, but only in accordance with the rule of law set forth by the U.S. Constitution. Unfortunately, Great Britain, France, and other Western nations have failed to get this message out in a timely fashion. We now witness what is happening in those countries as Islamic minorities, through violence and threat of violence, run amok.

On September 12, 2006, during a lecture at the University of Regensburg in Bavaria, Pope Benedict XVI quoted fourteenth-century Byzantine Emperor Manuel II Palaiologos: "Show me just what Muhammad brought that was new and there you will find things only evil and inhuman, such as his command to spread by the sword the faith he preached." The Pope made this comment in an academic lecture, comparing early Muslim teaching on religious freedom with the later teachings of jihadists. The Pope, expounding on the relationship between reason and Divine Nature, set forth that reason and faith go hand in hand, and that the concept of a holy war is always unreasonable and against the nature of God.

In response, radical Islamists worldwide erupted in violent protest: A nun was shot dead; a terrorist group linked to al Qaeda vowed to kill the Pope; and Christian churches in Palestine were attacked, proving the Pope's point.

In England, a lone and formidable voice of reason, Lord Carey, former Archbishop of Canterbury, noted that the world is witnessing a clash of civilizations. The archbishop quoted Samuel Huntington:

> Islam's borders are bloody and so are its innards. The fundamental problem for the West is not Islamic fundamentalism. It is Islam, a different civilisation whose people are convinced of the superiority of their culture and are obsessed with the inferiority of their power.[27]

Most other Westerners quickly condemned the Pope's comments and rushed to pacify the Islamists. No one dared defend the Christian faith or its adherents so violently attacked throughout the world; instead, they blamed the deaths on the Pope!

In France, such violence is often reported as youth violence in certain sectors where the police won't patrol and Sharia law prevails.

For decades, the United Kingdom tolerated plotting by domestic Islamists so long as they targeted other countries. Under the guise of freedom of speech, radical imams preached violence and extremism. They used that freedom to take over community organizations, mosques, and TV stations. The British MI-5 is now attempting to crack down on this activity, but, as a matter of simple demographics, it may be too late.

America should quickly come to a better arrangement with the Muslim world. Domestically, we can better protect our constitutional foundations, our heartland, and the rule of law. Internationally, such an arrangement or understanding with the Muslim world would cool tempers on both sides and allow for meaningful dialogue and improved trade and diplomacy. Pakistan in particular would understand this arrangement, as it has been dealing with China on this basis for some time. China builds ports, roads, and other infrastructure designed to increase trade and prosperity, yet does not meddle in Pakistan's internal affairs. Instead, America seems determined to meddle in other countries' affairs while simultaneously letting its guard down at home.

This is not a call for isolationism. Instead it is a call for realism over misguided idealism. The West is facing a threat as real and dangerous as Adolf Hitler's Nazi Germany, yet its strategic leaders flounder worse than the 1930s British parliament when it comes to identifying the threats and preparing to repel them. As Henry Kissinger recently stated in *Spiegel* when commenting on the failure of the Versailles Treaty and how it relates to events today: "The belief in democracy as a universal remedy regularly reappears in American foreign policy."[28] Such a well-intentioned but ultimately naïve belief consistently causes Western democracies to get sucker punched by more formidable realists in this Hobbesian world. While politicians can afford to tread down this path, our military must not. This is what is happening. Counterinsurgency (COIN) doctrine and trends toward peacekeeping and nation-building operations are being promoted at the expense of traditional force-on-force, combat operations.

When dealing with cultures and civilizations that understand the violent world of Hobbes better than soft power, the West can learn much from history. Before being quelled and absorbed by the greater Russian Empire in the nineteenth century, the Zaporozhian Cossacks resided in what is today central Ukraine. Toward the end of the seventeenth century, during one of their many skirmishes with the Islamists of the Ottoman Empire, these Cossacks received the following missive from Sultan Mehmet IV:

> I, Sultan Mohammed, Brother of the Sun and the Moon, Grandson and Vicar of God, Ruler of Kingdoms, Outstanding Knight, and Invincible Warrior, hereby order you Zaporozhzhian Cossacks: do obey my will unquestioningly and never again dare bother me with your raids!
>
> —Sultan Mehmet IV

The Cossacks replied.

> Thou Turkish Devil!
>
> Brother and companion to the accursed Devil, and Secretary to Lucifer himself, Greetings! What the hell kind of noble knight art thou? Satan voids and thy army devours. Never wilt thou be fit to have the sons of Christ under thee. Thy army we fear not, and by land and by sea in our chaikas we will do battle against thee.
>
> Thou scullion of Babylon, thou beer-brewer of Jerusalem, thou goat-thief of Alexandria, thou swineherd of Egypt both the Greater and the Lesser, thou Armenian pig and Tartar goat. Thou hangman of Kamyanets, thou evildoer of Podolia, thou great silly

oaf of all the world and of the netherworld and, before our God, a blockhead, a swine's snout, a mare's ass, and clown of Hades. May the devil take thee!

That is what the Cossacks have to say to thee, thou basest born of runts! Unfit art thou to lord it over true Christians! The date we know not, for no calendar have we got. The moon (month) is in the sky, the year is in a book, and the day is the same with us here as with ye over there—and thou can kiss us thou knowest where!
—Koshoviy Otaman Ivan Sirko and all
the Zaporozhian Cossack Brotherhood[29]

Instead of using any semblance of such direct and firm language, we plod along attempting appeasement after appeasement. From Barack Obama's June 2009 speech in Cairo to military decisions like not providing our warriors with the best footwear—pigskin boots—for fear that it would offend our Muslim brothers, the weak, vacillating messages we send curry no favor and present us simply as better targets.

In places like Jordan, Kuwait, and Morocco, there are signs of a true reformation within the Pan-Arabic Muslim world. This is important. The United States should actively encourage the continued blooming of modernity within those countries where the existence of a parliamentary system has acted as a moderating force on Islamist movements. Ray Takeyh and Nikolas K. Gvosdev describe the reformation:

The close of the twentieth and the beginning of the twenty-first century have also seen the transfer of power in much of the Muslim world to younger, better educated, more technocratic leaders—Mohammed VI of Morocco, Abdullah of Jordan, the rulers of the Gulf states and so on—who are actively seeking to create new forms of governance that can reconcile Islamic values and traditions while embracing political and economic modernity.[30]

There is a sharp distinction, however, between encouraging these types of Muslim nations and attempting to reconcile Sharia law with our Constitution and America's social contract with its citizens. Whereas many Western policy makers and strategists view culture as an obfuscating fog that must be cleared away before any meaningful political dialogue can occur, others, including most of the Islamic world, see culture as a defining virtue. To democratize Islam would most likely destroy what it means to be Islamic. And as a corollary, if we fail to hold fast to America's defining virtue—the primacy of individual liberties and private property rights—by continuing on a dangerous path toward European socialism, we may lose the power to prevail over Islam. This must not happen.

CHAPTER THREE

Turning the Law of War on Its Head

Just as the Supreme Court of the United States turned the First Amendment on its head with its rulings in the 1960s and 1970s concerning the free exercise of religion and speech, so too have American policy makers done with their misinterpretation and application of the Law of War. This must be understood and exposed for the dangerous fraud that it represents. Only then can America undergo a rigorous review of its policy objectives and how it conducts war. This will require a renewed reason that will better ensure a stronger military and a more enduring security and peace for its citizens.

The Law of War is the body of law, both codified and common, that concerns itself with the acceptable conduct of war. It addresses both *jus ad bellum*, the justifications for engaging in war, and *jus in bello*, acceptable wartime actions or conduct. Some of the central principles underlying the laws of war are that war should be limited to achieving the defined political goals that started the war; war should not include unnecessary destruction; and war should be ended as quickly as possible. Moreover, people and property not directly contributing to the war effort should be protected against unnecessary destruction and hardship. Certain persons and places—like noncombatants or civilians and hospitals, schools, and churches—are protected. These concepts have been codified over the years in diverse Geneva and Hague conventions and protocols.

America is floundering in her military efforts because the policy makers sending us on the missions ignore the demands of *jus ad bellum* and concurrently misinterpret the demands of *jus in bello*. Both of these errors accrue to our severe detriment in terms of American lives lost and ill-focused missions.

Jus Ad Bellum

Most of the conditions which must be met to satisfy the requirements for *jus ad bellum* are found in Grotius and derived from the writings of Saint Augustine, Saint Thomas Aquinas, and even works of classical antiquity. America's recent military adventures seemingly violate many of these legal maxims:

Just cause: There must be a just cause based on an injury received.

Fear with respect to a neighboring power is not a sufficient cause. For self-defense to be lawful it must be necessary; and it is not necessary unless we are certain, not only regarding the power of our neighbor, but also regarding his intention; the degree of certainty which is required is that which is accepted in morals.[31]

There is little doubt about the authority and moral justification for the United States to invade Afghanistan in 2001 in response to the attacks of September 11. There is continuing rationale and reasonable debate concerning the authority of the United States to invade Iraq in 2003. To continue in both locations, nine years after September 11, with aimless COIN operations with no apparent national interest or just cause, violates this concept.

Proportionality: Wars must be proportional to the costs entailed in prosecuting them. Ten billion dollars per month of U.S. taxpayers' money (in a nation cash-strapped and trillions of dollars in debt) to effect rampant death and destruction to no definable end makes you question our obeisance to this maxim.

Chance of success: There must be a reasonable chance of success. Again, the chances of turning Afghanistan into anything other than a tribal-based, nearly ungoverned region are laughable. Moreover, as discussed herein, the United States is the last country that should be involved in such attempts. Our mere presence pours salt into the festering wound of Islamism in the region.

Declaration of war: Nations must publicly declare their wars. Congress has not declared war since World War II, yet it keeps the appropriation bills flowing year after year. Seemingly no one will accept responsibility.

Legitimate authority: Only a legitimate authority may declare war. See above.

Last resort: War must always be a last resort. It is extremely hard to explain how nation-building at the point of a gun is the last resort.

Right intentions: No one knows America's intentions because we don't. We won't define our enemies; we refuse to apply overwhelming force even when we do; and our intentions change from one policy statement to the next. This is not to question the morality or will of our soldiers and commanders on the ground at the tip of the spear, but rather the elite policy makers who send them to their fate.

Jus in Bello

Once war has begun, the just war theory directs the conduct of combatants.

Distinction: Acts of war should be directed toward enemy combatants, not towards noncombatants caught in circumstances they did not create. Examples of prohibited acts include bombing civilian residential areas that include no military targets and committing acts of terrorism or reprisal against civilians. Our enemies in the current fight (and many past fights) ignore this rule with impunity, but the United States makes every effort to properly discern between combatants and noncombatants. Problems arise when our enemy does not wear a uniform and purposefully blends in and conducts acts of aggression from the civilian noncombatant community.

Proportionality: An attack should not be launched on a military objective if incidental civilian injuries—often referred to as "collateral damage"—would be clearly excessive in relation to the anticipated military advantage gained by the attack. Proportionality is of concern to commanders considering preplanned air or artillery strikes. It typically has little or nothing to do with the amount of force an individual or squad uses in response to an imminent threat of death or serious bodily injury.

Military necessity: An attack or action must be intended to help in the military defeat of the enemy, it must be an attack on a military objective, and the harm caused to civilians or civilian property must be proportional and not excessive in relation to the concrete and direct military advantage anticipated. This principle is meant to limit excessive and unnecessary death and destruction. By deliberately inserting our troops into the countryside of a tribal, Sharia culture, the United States is setting up an untenable and unnecessary tension between force protection and self-imposed tactical directives related to COIN. Moreover, misunderstanding and misapplication of the COIN doctrine itself has created an unreasonably and unnecessarily high legal standard for what constitutes reasonable interpretations of military necessity and proportionality.

In recent years, especially as the United States has become embroiled in and enamored with the counterinsurgency (COIN) fight, there has been a disturbing tendency to pervert long-held Law of War concepts so that they are used both by our enemies as offensive weapons and, unwittingly, by ourselves against our own cause. When the enemy misuses a protected place—utilizing a mosque as an ammunition supply point, for instance—we never claim the enemy is responsible. Instead, we blame ourselves when one of our units destroys the mosque. More disturbingly, when the enemy uses civilians as shields and initiates an attack on U.S. forces, we berate—even court-martial—our soldiers for returning fire.

The insanity, however, does not stop there. Recently, in Iraq, a soldier shot and killed an insurgent who had fired his weapon at a coalition outpost. A brigade judge advocate—a newly minted *funded legal education program* (FLEP) officer and former infantry officer to boot—advised the brigade commander that the soldier's use of force was unlawful because "the insurgent's shot was way over the head of the Soldier's position and was not sufficient indicia of hostile intent!" More frightening than this ridiculous advice was the fact the brigade commander listened to the judge advocate. Commanders, fearful of the repercussions of suspected Law of War violations, have in many circumstances abdicated their commands to their legal advisors. Unfortunately, the same thing happened in 2010 in Marjah, Afghanistan:

> "I understand the reason behind it, but it's so hard to fight a war like this," said Lance Corp. Travis Anderson, 20, from Altoona,

Iowa. "They're using our rules of engagement against us," he said, adding that his platoon had repeatedly seen men dropping their guns into ditches before walking away to melt among civilians.[32]

In essence, we are rewarding the *muj* for their violations of the Law of War. Political correctness, in the guise of the COIN fight, is going to get more troops killed in an ultimately losing effort. And in an ever-frenzied attempt to "gain the moral high ground" and "win their hearts and minds," we let the enemy continue to inflict death by a thousand cuts.

This is not surprising when you stop to think about recent developments in the way in which America's wars are being fought. We no longer apply the fundamentals of the Law of War to our combat actions just as we no longer brutally route out and kill the enemy. In fact, you'd be hard-pressed to get our current leadership to define exactly who our enemy is. We cannot call our fight the "war on terror" anymore; it is an "overseas contingency operation." While the change from "war on terror" is technically correct—it should be a "war on terrorists" as "terrorism" is a tactic—the redefining of the terms of debate removes the passion, zeal, and the grounding sacrifice of our warriors. It also has the unintended consequence of relegating that statistically minute portion of our population that is actually defending our country (the armed forces) to the status of third-class citizens without a voice. We certainly cannot call anyone the enemy, as that term interferes with the Pollyanna world view of the current administration.

In both Iraq and Afghanistan we have transitioned to a Law Enforcement Model (LEM). In both countries (with the minor exception of an extremely small special operations task force), a commander must petition the governing country to get a warrant to go after the bad guys. This so-called "warrant-based targeting" requires United States soldiers and marines—the guarantors of the only freedoms extant in these Third World hellholes—to petition the host nation government, hat in hand, and politely ask if they wouldn't too terribly mind if we went out and hunted down their enemies for them. Again, this would be funny were it not for the death and mutilation being wrought upon our warriors every single day by the very savages for which our warriors need warrants to kill. Our leaders need to search their souls each time they bury a hero or see a soldier, sailor, airman, or marine who has been wounded, blinded, or maimed in some horrific manner. They should examine whether they have done everything they possibly could to ensure our forces apply overwhelming violence against the enemy, win this war quickly, and come home safely.

One of the impetuses for writing this book was a news story of an airline captain who held the passengers in their seats so that the family of an Army Private, the body of whom was in the cold-belly of the airliner being transported home for the last time, could disembark in time to see their son being removed from the plane. This story brought tears to the authors' eyes. We as a country think we are doing our part when we let the families of our fallen warriors off a plane first or when we put little yellow ribbons on the backs of our vehicles to show we care. These acts demonstrate concern no more than putting a "Free Tibet" bumper sticker on the back of a vehicle, its driver never having the inclination to ever travel to Tibet and fight for the Tibetans' freedom.

The sad but true adage oft-repeated within the services is that the military went to war, and America went shopping. This is not meant to denigrate the heartfelt support offered by many, but rather to implore America to stand up and demand better leadership and direction from its senior leaders when the blood of its sons and daughters is being sacrificed on a daily basis.

The LEM currently in place in the COIN environment works if we are in control of the spheres in which we attempt to influence conduct. Law enforcement is a good technique for solving crimes and doling out retribution—in other words finding those responsible for violating societal norms and imposing punishment on them as a deterrent to those similarly inclined. Using the LEM—with its concomitant guarantees of constitutional protections, federal habeas review, and an all-too-willing cadre of fifth columnists comprised of the ACLU and various liberal progressive intellectuals—may work in polite Western-industrialized societies, but it is an entirely wrongheaded way to fight a war. Whether we were aware of it or not, America has been in a state of war with al Qaeda since the late 1970s. Treating these insidious vipers as mere criminals led directly to September 11. Even after that supposed cataclysmic event, some of our most prominent politicians either are willfully ignorant or too stupid to understand the difference between a crime and an act of war.

In the presidential debates of 2004, Massachusetts senator John Kerry parroted this type of thinking by stating that he would issue orders "to have bin Laden arrested." This statement is what passes for critical thinking of an enlightened sort among the political class. The fact that we as a nation even tolerate such woeful ignorance on wartime matters is inexcusable. Kerry's line of thinking was an echo of the thinking from the early days of the Clinton administration wherein the "wonder kids" of the new political class would solve the world's problems by flying C-130s off the deck of aircraft carriers and former UN Ambassador Madeleine Albright installed as Secretary of State would spread her policy of militant adventurism about the world; and many other follies.

Such idealism is incorrect and dangerous. The militant adventurism of the Clinton administration started us down the slippery slope of forced democratization. On this slope, we lost our focus and many of our grounding values. There is only one way to fight a war: call it a war and fight! Wars have been around for centuries, and an entire body of law was developed to ensure we can attack and vanquish our foes while causing minimal destruction to innocent civilians. We adhere to this construct; our enemies don't.

The law may direct the conduct of war, but looking to the law for all answers is dangerous. The primary goal of all warring nations is to ensure national survival. We can preach about the moral high ground all we want, but the first order of the day is to win the war, not adhere to a rule of law. If we lose the war and our way of life is severely diminished as a result of trying to ensure the world likes us by hamstringing our war effort, the effort may not have been prudent.

As attorneys, we are asked all the time what the law says on a particular issue. We have worked with various entities within the military, and we know there are often no regulations that describe the sphere of conduct allowed within a particular realm. The possibilities are far too random and abstruse to fall under the handy rubric of an Army Regulation or a Department of Defense Instruction. This is where good operational lawyers make their money: by comparing and contrasting to like or similar situations. Barring clear guidance of allowed and prohibited conduct, lawyers must analogize to current laws and regulations in place and make arguments for the adoption or extension of an applicable construct as precedent in getting to yes for the warriors. The following chapters explain how this very commodity makes lawyers in the defense establishment so dangerous. Bottom line: most miss the first and most important lesson—war is about killing the enemy!

If law were a simple construct, the Supreme Court would not need nine justices. One justice could simply refer to the manual and render an opinion out of its pages. But the law is neither static nor simple. Reasonable minds will differ as to the meaning of a particular statute or the construction of a particular section of the United States Code. Constitutional scholars encompass the entire political spectrum from the extreme left to the far right. Hence, nine justices are needed to vigorously argue constitutional construction, statutory interpretation, and at times, societal engineering. There is no mathematical equivalent to what the law is.

One of the dangers of relying on lawyers to dictate warfighting capability is that lawyers are—for the most part—a product of their experiences. There are few lawyers within the military who comprehend the dynamics of a deadly force encounter. As set forth later in this book, all sorts of "talismanic incantations" are uttered to try to camouflage what many try to pass off as critical reasoning. Part of Army judge advocates' continuing professional education requires them to obtain a Master of Laws (LLM), an advanced professional degree above and beyond a Juris Doctorate. These legal Marplots—like the officious meddlers in Centlivre's *The Busy Body*—are all the more contemptible because most military lawyers are far more educated than their civilian counterparts.

Unfortunately, many lawyers confuse education with intelligence. They may be highly educated and adequately grasp and understand federal rules of criminal procedure, but they are uncomfortable—to say the least—with the up close and violent business of killing people. Hence, they hesitate when discussing the lawfulness of a JDAM (Joint Direct Attack Munition, or precision-guided bomb) strike in a populated area. They simply are not trained to have a ready method of analysis in which to default in the realm of killing.

Part of the reason for this failure is competition for scant resources. As Napoleon told his commanders: "I can give you everything you need, but I can't give you more time." After instituting an effective Law of War program at the Joint Readiness Training Center as an "Observer-Controller" at Fort Polk, author Patterson was assigned to the Army Judge Advocate General's School in order to pursue his LLM degree. While there, he was asked by the schoolhouse to develop a program to teach JAG basic course students (lawyers entering the army and receiving basic military legal education) how to operate within a brigade throughout the spectrum of warfare.

After spending innumerable hours with talented staff putting together lesson plans, logistics, programs of instruction, and cost estimates, the end
result was a two-week culmination exercise for basic course students
wherein they would live in GP-Mediums (tents) and handle the basic
issues that would arise with a surly commander in an uncertain environment. The two weeks required to adequately train the basic course students
was summarily rejected by JAGC leadership at the School. The team was
asked to go back to the drawing board and redesign something less time
intensive. After a tremendous amount of cutting, the course was whittled
down to one week of bare-bones issues that a student must master in order
to be effective at the brigade level. Once again, the team was told to go
back and come up with something less time intensive.

As you can guess, the team smartly saluted and redrafted all documents, goals, and knowledge requirements. The course got knocked down
to two days, then one day, and then the team was asked to put something
together for a four-hour period "after hours" block of instruction. In other
words, the JAGC leadership at the schoolhouse wanted something that
briefed well, but they were not willing to put forth the effort to fund it. This
is one reason why judge advocates are often unsure of the advice provided
by JAGC doctrine.

Nowadays, into the tenth year of what appears to be an interminable
war, the army has alleviated some of these training issues. But it still has
major problems. We still do not adequately train our young judge advocates for the positions we are thrusting them into before we send them into
combat. No commander would ask his infantry to clear a trench line without having trained them in the crawl-walk-run methodology. Why then
would the legal community send young lawyers into the fog of war not
having been trained to the utmost extent possible?

The answer is that our doctrine writers are woefully ignorant of what
passes for frontline duty nowadays. We take a young captain and put him
in a brigade and call him an operational lawyer. Calling him so doesn't
make him so. Lawyers simply don't know what they don't know—if they
don't know the "mins," safety zones, saturation density, and failure rate for
a given set of FASCAM (Family of Scatterable Mines), how can they intel-
ligently advise the commander on the legality or risk of the targeting?

What is unforgiveable is that a cadre of senior judge advocates routinely admonishes young lawyers against going "native." This is especially

reprehensible in light of the fact that lawyers must be admitted to a state bar to be eligible to practice law in the military. State bar ethics rules require that an attorney educate himself to the needs and business of the client so as to provide competent and professional advice. So then why do we have senior military lawyers decrying and admonishing their subordinates for going native, which is really doing that which their respective bars mandate?

Another problem emanates from certain elements of the Judge Advocate General's Corps of the services who fancy themselves as internationalists. These pipe-smoking intellectuals were never warriors, and they despise those who are. At conferences these former and current military attorneys disparage some operationally savvy judge advocates as being complicit in war crimes for advising on absolutely legal detainee interrogation methods.

So if we, as judge advocates, can't figure out how and, more importantly, *what* to train, how do we expect young lawyers to adequately advise commanders on critical legal principles? Further cloud the battlefield with unclear and confusing guidance from our civilian masters and the incentive for young lawyers to rush to the sound of the guns is seriously eroded because a criminal indictment, rather than a victory parade, may await.

The Law of War mandates that we protect our nation first and foremost. The LEM is an inappropriate construct for the military to champion. That we have allowed countries we invaded to dictate to us the means and methods by which we defend them is absurd to the rank and file taking the bullets. Why can't our leadership comprehend this?

The extension of Geneva Convention protections to al Qaeda is lunacy of the highest order. Geneva Conventions are treaties that apply only to international armed conflict between the high contracting parties that have signed them. Al Qaeda is neither a nation-state nor a contracting party to the convention; therefore, it is not entitled to convention protections. Members of al Qaeda do not carry arms openly, wear a recognizable uniform or readily identified insignia, conduct operations in accordance with the Law of War, or hold themselves accountable to a chain of command or political construct. Al Qaeda does not take prisoners, does not limit warfare to combatants, and does not spare innocent civilian life. But in the quest to hold ourselves to a higher standard (not sure whom we are trying to impress other than the French or Amnesty International) we—as a matter of policy—extend Geneva Convention protections to these savages. Let's not try to do it halfway. If we are going to apply Geneva Convention protections to the *muj* and reward them for violation of the Law of War, then let's do what the Geneva Convention mandates: establish canteens from which they can purchase sundries, pay them in Swiss francs for details performed, ask them no more than limited information for reporting and accountability reasons, and repatriate them at the conclusion of hostilities. We challenge any politician or military leader to adopt these standards to their full extent.

The common refrain that we must afford them Geneva Convention protections or our warriors will be at peril in future conflicts is hollow, disingenuous, and dangerously ignorant to the point of criminality. Never have our troops been afforded Geneva Convention protections in a conflict: not in Korea, North Vietnam, the first Gulf War, the Balkans, the second Gulf War, or with the Taliban or al Qaeda.

Let's look to future hotspots and likely adversaries. Pick an area: China, Russia, Venezuela, Sudan, Yemen, or the Horn of Africa. If our political class and military leaders insist on affording Geneva Convention status to illegal combatants or entities not privileged under the Law of War in the vain hope that our enemies will afford our troops comity in the Geneva Convention realm, they are seriously uneducable.

The fantasy that our determined enemies—hard-core Islamic extremists—will abide by international rules of law is compounded by some Western policy makers' slavish adherence to every ridiculous utterance that emanates from the International Committee of the Red Cross (ICRC). A prime example is that organization's attempt to distinguish between combatants and noncombatants in this era of asymmetric warfare and attacks by an enemy who refuses to wear a uniform. The ICRC correctly notes that "civilians lose protection against direct attack for the duration of each specific act amounting to direct participation in hostilities." Unfortunately, and this is where the ICRC demonstrates its woeful ignorance of the ways of man and combat, it goes on to say in an attempt to define the beginning and end of direct participation in hostilities, "Measures preparatory to the execution of a specific act of direct participation in hostilities, as well as the deployment to and the return from the location of its execution, constitute an integral part of that act," implying that a *muj* can attack U.S. forces, kill innocent civilians, and so long as we don't kill him immediately he can then go back to driving his taxicab and be safe from kinetic strikes.[33] Such fuzzy-headed logic may make sense while safely sipping lattes in Geneva, but is anathema to the successful prosecution of counter-terrorism.

Once again we see our political masters tying our hands behind our backs and the senior military leadership acquiescing on the matter. If "The United States has never in its history consented to the idea that the laws of war protect terrorists,"[34] why then are we continually shooting ourselves in the face? Whether it's the enemy, the terrain, the laws and policy to apply, or the method of warfare, our leadership picks the option most restrictive and limiting to our armed forces. This insanity must stop. Our senior military leaders need to speak forcefully and consistently to our civilian masters in this regard.

The Detention Issues

What enables the wise sovereign and the good general to strike and conquer, and achieve things beyond the reach of ordinary men is *foreknowledge*. Now this foreknowledge cannot be elicited from spirits; it cannot be obtained inductively from experience, nor by any deductive calculation. Knowledge of the enemy's disposition can only be obtained from other men.[35]

—Sun Tzu

The intelligence community of the United States can't figure out how to glean information from persons detained in this war on terror. The enemy has learned to use information operations and lawfare against us in this realm perhaps even more so than on the kinetic or killing front. The Obama administration has attempted to close down Guantanamo Bay (GITMO) and send many unlawful combatants to their home countries, only to return later at an alarming, but not so surprising, rate to once again wage war against us.

The Obama administration's decision to close the Department of Defense's detention facility at GITMO and to continue to limit the scope of interrogation techniques is predicated on a blend of political, policy, and legal concerns surrounding the treatment of detainees, some legitimate and some not. Consider the lens through which most Western lawyers, ethicists, and politicians look when defining torture:

> What constitutes degradation and humiliation to a pampered citizen of a Western democracy may seem trivial to a person brought up in harsh conditions in the Third World. We need to challenge the conventional assumption that discomforts and inconveniences are all inhuman, cruel and unacceptable. A tough, trained, rehearsed, young terrorist has advantages over a prisoner accustomed to Western comforts. And the Jihadist has probably been well briefed on countering interrogation and on the constraints within which a Western interrogator must work.[36]

Failing to understand this cultural distinction, many lawyers providing guidance on the detention issue substitute their personal notions of propriety. However, an attorney providing operational legal guidance to a commander should give guidance that is easily understood and free from personal bias. While the average military interrogator probably should be prohibited from using enhanced interrogation techniques such as waterboarding, the rules adopted for other government agencies, and certain special mission units, should be based on law and reason rather than emotion or personal bias. Too much guidance on this topic flows from polite Western notions of what constitutes torture.

However, let us look at the United States Law, 18 U.S.C. 2340, to learn exactly what torture is:

> (1) "torture" means an act committed by a person acting under the color of law specifically intended to inflict severe physical or mental pain or suffering (other than pain or suffering incidental to lawful sanctions) upon another person within his custody or physical control;

> (2) "severe mental pain or suffering" means the prolonged mental harm caused by or resulting from—

> (A) the intentional infliction or threatened infliction of severe physical pain or suffering;

(B) the administration or application, or threatened administration or application, of mind-altering substances or other procedures calculated to disrupt profoundly the senses or the personality;

(C) the threat of imminent death; or

(D) the threat that another person will imminently be subjected to death, severe physical pain or suffering, or the administration or application of mind-altering substances or other procedures calculated to disrupt profoundly the senses or personality; and

(3) "United States" means the several States of the United States, the District of Columbia, and the commonwealths, territories, and possessions of the United States.

The statute is fairly clear, and this is what we mean when we use the word "torture" in this chapter. There is room for legitimate discussion surrounding just what "intentional infliction" or "severe physical or mental pain" mean.

First of all, we as a country do not torture. There was no secret policy directly from President Bush or Vice President Cheney ordering the torture of detainees. Contrary to popular belief and the constant mantra of the press that Abu Ghraib was a policy decision of the Bush administration, it was, in fact, the direct result of a grossly incompetent commander, Brigadier General Janice Karpinski, being placed in a position for which she was completely unqualified. Her failure to exercise even the basic rudiments of leadership by failing to conduct inspections led to an *Animal House* atmosphere within the confines of the prison. The behavior exhibited by the soldiers within her command, while neither condoned nor excused, is easily explained via the psychological phenomenon of moral disengagement. Moral disengagement is a validated condition wherein good people end up doing bad things. At the risk of oversimplification, it is the devolution of a functioning environment into a *Lord of the Flies* atmosphere. Proper leadership and applying the basics of command responsibility would have prevented such behavior.

But however bad Abu Ghraib was, it was not torture. Nor was it United States policy directed from the highest levels as some progressives would have us believe. Unfortunately, the only people to pay the price for this gross dereliction of duty were some lower ranking soldiers. To indict Karpinski for her dereliction of duty, notably documented in the many investigations arising out of Abu Ghraib, would be further indictment of the military's social experimentation and political correctness.

Giving detainees adequate nutrition and hydration and allowing them to sleep eight hours in a twenty-four-hour period ensures that we don't overstep the bounds of the torture statute. Questioning someone for hours at a time and making them somewhat uncomfortable, however, clearly does not rise to the level of torture as defined by the statute and common sense. No one should argue that torture should be used or freely allowed as a method of warfare. But there are those who resort to the very tactic that has enabled the *muj* to penetrate our most secure organizations, changing the terms of the debate. If you fail to actually define what torture is and merely rail against "torture," you will get mass agreement from across the political spectrum. After all, who is for torture? But when you break it down to the facts, the argument gets fuzzy. Can we keep someone awake for sixteen hours if we allow them to have eight hours of sleep? Can we give them two four-hour sleep periods in a twenty-four-hour period? Can we play loud music at them to prolong capture shock? (*muj* hate music—it could lead to dancing and other perverted Western habits.) How thick must the mattress and bedroll be to ensure a level of comfort that is not consistent with what some may label abuse or torture?

These are all legitimate questions and should frame the debate. Rather than engage in the debate, our leadership merely reverts to the lowest common denominator to ensure we treat people to a standard wherein *nobody* could argue that we are bad people. This is not applying the rule of law as envisioned by the framers of the Geneva Conventions, but rather following a rule of perception in an information-operation world dominated by our enemies, both foreign and domestic.

Recently some legal scholars and essayists have gone to extremes in their condemnation of the Bush administration's policy concerning enhanced interrogation techniques. For instance they have pointed to the prosecution of Japanese captors for use of water torture techniques as a basis for outlawing our use of "waterboarding."[37] Or they attempt to draw a moral or legal equivalency between the types of torture inflicted upon John McCain and his fellow POWs by the North Vietnamese (or those inflicted by our current adversaries) and waterboarding. These arguments are disingenuous for a number of reasons.

The Japanese were prosecuted after the war for the systemic, repeated, and long-term starvation, mutilation, and killings of Allied POWs: Their use of water torture was merely a small cog in their wheel of depravity. Nothing in the manner by which the United States has treated captured terrorists today compares with the Japanese cruelties during World War II. As it relates to torture, performing a fifteen-second simu- lated drowning upon an individual is the same type of interrogation tech- nique to which some of our own special operations forces and aviators have been subjected when they endured Survival Evasion Resistance Escape (SERE) training. Waterboarding was only used by one of the two Navy Resistance Training Laboratories and has been discontinued. The only SOF forces who had been exposed were SEALs. More aviators were exposed than SEALs. Moreover, there is a qualitative and legal difference between its use in training, where a student has at least some clear ability to stop the experience, and having it done to a captive. Perhaps most importantly, however, there have been no substantive allegations that Department of Defense interrogators ever used waterboarding on de- tainees. Moreover, waterboarding in no way compares to the monstrous wanton burning, flaying, breaking of limbs, and decapitations that radical jihadists routinely impose upon their captives. Nor can it in any way be equated with the real torture experienced by U.S. prisoners of war in World War II, the Korean War, the Vietnam War, or even in Iraqi hands during the 1991 war to liberate Kuwait, during which the International Committee of the Red Cross turned a blind eye to the torture of U.S. and Allied prisoners of war.

It's troubling that some lawyers cannot spot such distinctions, and the rhetoric masquerading as legal analysis by those who wish to politicize this matter should be ignored as it only serves to cloud the otherwise mundane truth surrounding the operational applications of legal doctrine. Many attorneys, including, unfortunately, some affiliated with the services' legal centers and schools, have voiced the opinion that members of the Bush administration's Defense and Justice Departments, as well as some serving judge advocates, should be investigated and possibly charged with war crimes for their policies surrounding the interrogation issues.[38] The fact that a group of current and former judge advocates, including a former

Judge Advocate General of the Army and law school dean and the Executive Director of the Army Legal Center and School, would attend a conference and opine in such a manner is noteworthy. Such rhetoric distracts from sound operational and strategic legal advice focused on critically thinking about what works and is lawful.

Just look at the arguments over the treatment of some of the September 11 masterminds captured and detained at Guantanamo Bay (GITMO). We have, in essence, extended Geneva Convention and international Law of War privileges to unlawful combatants—the very people the Geneva Conventions were designed *not* to protect! Historically stateless terrorists and other similarly situated bad actors have not been entitled to the protections that this administration has afforded to them pursuant to Common Article 3 of the Geneva Conventions:

> As the eminent military historian Sir Michael Howard argued shortly after 9/11, the status of al Qaeda terrorists is to be found in a distinction first made by the Romans and subsequently incorporated into international law by way of medieval and early modern European jurisprudence. According to Mr. Howard, the Romans distinguished between bellum (war against *legitimus hostis*, a legitimate enemy) and *guerra* (war against *latrunculi*, pirates, robbers, brigands and outlaws).
>
> Bellum became the standard for interstate conflict, and it is here that the Geneva Conventions were meant to apply. They do not apply to *guerra*. Indeed, punishment for *latrunculi*, "the common enemies of mankind," traditionally has been summary execution.[39]

The most amazing thing about the GITMO issue that has gone unnoticed by most politicians and mainstream media is that despite the fact that most of the detainees should never have been afforded protections under the Geneva Conventions, moreover the wider protections of Common Article 3, GITMO itself has complied with Common Article 3 provisions. The relevant portion of the Secretary of Defense Memorandum, "Review of Department Compliance with President's Executive Order on Detainee Conditions of Confinement, dated 2 February 2009," as set forth below, was in response to an Obama administration order soon after Obama took office. It bears careful reading:

After considerable deliberation and a comprehensive review, it is our judgment that the conditions of confinement in Guantánamo are in conformity with Common Article 3 of the Geneva Conventions.

In our view, there are two components in the scope of the compliance review taken from Common Article 3: the first is the explicit prohibition against specified acts (at any time and at any place). Any substantiated evidence of prohibited acts discovered in the course of the review would have warranted a finding of "non-compliance" with Common Article 3. We found no such evidence.

Additionally, determining conformity with Common Article 3 requires examination of the directive aspect of the Article, this being that "Persons . . . shall in all circumstances be treated humanely." This element of the effort demanded that the Review Team examine conditions of detention based upon our experience and professional backgrounds, informed and challenged by outside commentary. As a result of that effort, we find that the conditions of confinement in Guantánamo also meet the directive requirements of Common Article 3 of the Geneva Conventions.

While we conclude that conditions at Guantánamo are in conformity with Common Article 3, from our review, it was apparent that the chain of command responsible for the detention mission at Guantánamo consistently seeks to go beyond a minimalist approach to compliance with Common Article 3, and endeavors to enhance conditions in a manner as humane as possible consistent with security concerns.

The U.S. military goes to great effort to pamper and not offend Muslim detainees. Detainees are provided cable television, Internet access, a full library, and rich diet. When detainees are given Western newspapers to read, prison guards are forced to take a magic marker to each page to blacken out any exposed skin on the arms and legs of models in the advertisements so as not to offend the terrorists. The detention facility is so well regulated that an ICRC visitor commented that it is the best run and most humane facility she had ever seen. Even though in full compliance with even the most restrictive interpretation of international law, our senior policy leaders still feel compelled to apologize to the world for treating terrorists this way. Such apologies, while perhaps gaining President Obama admiration in the salons of Europe, gain us nothing in our relations with the Islamic world. We are, as bin Laden predicted, simply seen as weak and vacillating.

Just how far both external and internal enemies have used lawfare against us can best be viewed through the not-so-distant mirror of the Supreme Court case of *Johnson v. Eisentrager*, 339 U.S. 763 (1950), wherein the great Associate Justice Robert H. Jackson—an FDR appointee—scoffed at the notion of granting habeas corpus rights to a non-U.S. person not on U.S. soil (in this case German POWs being held in the Far East):

> Such trials would hamper the war effort and bring aid and comfort to the enemy. They would diminish the prestige of our commanders, not only with enemies but with wavering neutrals. It would be difficult to devise more effective fettering of a field commander than to allow the very enemies he is ordered to reduce to submission to call him to account in his own civil courts and divert his efforts and attention from the military offensive abroad to the legal defensive at home. Nor is it unlikely that the result of such enemy litigiousness would be a conflict between judicial and military opinion highly comforting to enemies of the United States.

Not surprisingly, the Bush administration relied upon such sound precedent when setting up the GITMO detention facility. But by a 5-4 split decision in 2006, the Supreme Court reversed *Eisentrager* and granted habeas corpus rights to unlawful enemy combatants. Now enemy litigiousness is at an all-time high. And military commanders in both Iraq and Afghanistan are worried about the judicialization of their targeting processes. One must wonder at the success a U.S. litigant would have in a Taliban-run *shura*!

(Not) Hunting the Enemy

On the pre-capture or active kinetic hunting and killing front, we have unnecessarily ceded the moral high ground to the enemy as well. When *muj* fire at us from crowds using civilian shields, as they did in Somalia and continue to do in Iraq and Afghanistan, we bend over backwards apologizing to the world when civilians are killed in the cross fire. Even more frighteningly, some commanders attempt to forbid or limit our forces from returning fire in self-defense. We should be prosecuting the enemy—those we don't kill—for war crimes and hanging them as we did the Japanese and Nazis after the Second World War. Instead we hamstring our own warriors and then prosecute them when they exercise legitimate military operations.

To make clear who holds responsibility, an analogy to domestic criminal law is in order. If a bank robber fires at responding law enforcement officers during the course of a robbery and a bank teller is killed in the ensuing gunfight, the bank robber is liable for murder regardless of whether the offending bullet was fired from his gun or a cop's gun. This is known as the felony murder rule in most states. The same concept applies in the Law of War: That faction who violates the Law of War is responsible for the death and destruction that results. If the *muj* use a mosque or hospital to store ammunition, the mosque loses its protected status under the Law of War and becomes targetable. The *muj* should then be held legally responsible for its destruction if we target it.

In response to this reasonable and lawful interpretation of international law, the cry may be, "We can't cause civilian deaths or shoot mosques or we will lose the hearts and minds of the people!" The flaw in such logic is that, in the long run, the hearts and minds of the people in a Muslim culture will never be in accord with a transient, outside Western force. They may be for a while so long as there is a strong security presence. But the indigenous population knows that sooner or later the United States will tire of the fight, and they will have to live with whatever hegemonic force remains: Taliban, Shiite, or tribal warlord.

Perhaps most frightening is how such lawfare is blunting our warrior ethos and turning U.S. forces against themselves through command and control by investigation. Too many times, in an effort to prove to those who do not really care (the Taliban, the Afghan government, and even sometimes the EU), the United States military embarks upon labyrinthine investigations into the combat actions of its own soldiers based upon specious complaints of captured al Qaeda operatives. This occurs despite the fact that such enemy tactics, to include self-infliction of wounds, are spelled out in diverse al Qaeda training manuals.

Currently, it is a proven tactic, technique, and procedure (TTP) for our enemies to claim they have been tortured at every point in their detention journey. This tactic is reinforced by our politically correct leadership overseeing the military launching an investigation for every complaint. A *muj* can get rolled up or detained in Mosul and spend the day at a holding cell before being transferred to Baghdad. Upon arrival in Baghdad he will say he was tortured at Mosul. The first investigation is started. Then upon processing and transfer from Baghdad into a division holding facility he will claim another set of torture at Baghdad. The military then initiates the second investigation. By the time he is enrolled in a detainee facility he will have been through three or four holding facilities. The detainee claims he was tortured at each facility thereby launching multiple investigations that are often ill-coordinated, redundant, and mutually exclusive.

In Baghdad, an Army Criminal Investigation Division (CID) agent in exasperation vented about the guidance he was given to clear his case log of hundreds of cases. The CID brass at Fort Gillem, Georgia, (safely ensconced back in the States, none of whom at the time had deployed) directed him to personally interview each claimant. When the agent told the Fort Gillem brass that many of these detainees had been released and were back in heavily enemy-populated cities such as Fallujah, in al Anbar province, the brass handled the situation as if it were a domestic law enforcement investigation. They opened their guidebook to look up the answer to "how to interview claimants" and they then instructed the agent to go to Fallujah and canvas the neighborhoods door-to-door looking for the alleged victims to validate their claims. And this happened during the heavily contested offensive in Fallujah in November 2004. This CID agent was one of the good guys and was a thorough professional. We cannot say the same thing for his superiors.

While investigation is important for purposes of discipline and maintaining general obeisance to the Law of War, we are investigating our warriors to the point of absurdity and severely dulling the sharp point of our military spear. This is well voiced in a letter written by Representative Dan Burton to Major General Charles Cleveland, Commander, Special Operations Command Central, concerning that command's prosecution of three Navy SEALs for allegedly mistreating a captured Islamic terrorist.

DAN BURTON
5TH DISTRICT, INDIANA

COMMITTEES:

FOREIGN AFFAIRS
SUBCOMMITTEES:
MIDDLE EAST AND SOUTH ASIA
RANKING MEMBER
WESTERN HEMISPHERE
FORMER CHAIRMAN

OVERSIGHT AND GOVERNMENT
REFORM
FORMER CHAIRMAN
SUBCOMMITTEES:
NATIONAL SECURITY AND FOREIGN AFFAIRS
DOMESTIC POLICY

Congress of the United States
House of Representatives
Washington, DC 20515-1405

WASHINGTON OFFICE:
2308 RAYBURN HOUSE OFFICE BUILDING
WASHINGTON, DC 20515-1405
TELEPHONE: (202) 225-2276

DISTRICT OFFICES:
8900 KEYSTONE AT THE CROSSING
INDIANAPOLIS, IN 46240
TELEPHONE: (317) 848-0201
TOLL-FREE: (800) 382-6020

209 SOUTH WASHINGTON STREET
MARION, IN 46952
TELEPHONE: (765) 662-6770
TOLL-FREE: (877) 846-2936

www.house.gov/burton

January 4, 2010

Major General Charles T. Cleveland
Commander, Special Operations Command Central
U.S. Central Command
7115 South Boundary Boulevard
MacDill AFB, FL 33621-5101

Dear General Cleveland:

I received your letter of December 15, 2009, regarding the pending courts-martial of Petty Officers Huertas, McCabe and Keefe; and I appreciate your office's attempting to set the record straight and clarify what you describe as the "incomplete and factually inaccurate" press coverage of the situation. Having reviewed all of the material you provided, I still have to strongly disagree with the decision of your officers to pursue punishment of these Navy SEALs.

Ahmed Hashim Abed was one of the most wanted terrorists in Iraq; responsible for the murders of innocent American civilians and numerous attacks on American and coalition forces. The injuries to Mr. Abed were, as you readily admit, relatively minor and certainly pale in comparison to the brutality of the crimes he helped perpetrate. While Petty Officers Huertas, McCabe and Keefe may have been wrong to not fully cooperate with investigators, it seems to me that the punishment still far exceeds the crime. In my opinion, prosecutorial discretion should have been exercised.

Beyond the fates of the three individual sailors, I have some general concerns about this case that are only reinforced by your letter. First, the fact that fellow U.S. service personnel initially raised the accusations against Petty Officers Huertas, McCabe and Keefe strongly suggests that we have created a culture within our Armed Forces where our military personnel are now more concerned about protecting themselves from legal jeopardy for every action or statement, than they are about fighting the enemy. Our troops and these SEALs need to be bold and decisive in combat; not hesitant and over-thinking every action for fear of prosecution. We are in a war that we must win against a determined, patient enemy who already believes we do not have the will to do what is necessary to defeat them.

Second, because of the intensive media coverage of this case – even if it is incomplete and factually inaccurate as you describe, this is the public's perception of the case – the American people are outraged by the courts-martial of individuals who should be hailed as heroes. In fact, over 30,000 Americans have signed my online petition calling for an end to this prosecution. Perhaps even more alarming than the decline in morale this case has caused the country is the boost in morale and confidence that this case gives to Al Qaeda terrorists, who as I said, already believe America does not have the will or stomach to do what is necessary to defeat them.

General Cleveland, you are a distinguished soldier and former Special Forces operator yourself. I have the utmost respect for you personally. In this case the American people's perception is that you are unfairly prosecuting three heroes based, at least in part, upon the word of an inhumane monster. Al-Qaeda's own handbook instructs their operatives to allege detainee abuse if detained by American forces. In fact, al-Qaeda operatives are trained to self-inflict injuries for the sole purpose of accusing U.S. forces of abuse. We've seen repeated cases of this since the conflicts in Iraq and Afghanistan began. In my opinion, carrying forward these courts-martial will do our Nation and our Armed Forces more harm than good. I respectfully and strongly urge you to exercise your leadership authority, stop the impending trials and drop the charges against these American heroes.

I await your prompt response.

Sincerely,

Dan Burton
Member of Congress

CC: Hon. Barack Obama, Hon. Robert Gates, Adm. Mike Mullen

Investigations of soldiers for what are empirically lawful acts as a leadership tool or to prove to our enemies—who don't care anyway—that we follow the supposed rule of law causes soldiers to hesitate in using force, unnecessarily placing them at greater risk. As FBI studies have shown, hesitation in the face of a threat unduly increases risk of death or serious injury to our own forces. Missions are dangerous enough without this type of investigative grandstanding.

Apache attack helicopter battalion commanders, afraid of allegations of excessive force, will now not allow their pilots to engage suspected enemy positions unless the aircraft's gun cameras are functioning to preserve evidence of hostile acts and appropriate response. Not that Dirty Harry movies often provide good legal guidance, but Clint Eastwood's quote, "When I see a naked man with a butcher knife and a hard-on chasing a women down an alley, I don't exactly think he is collecting for the Red Cross," is all the legal analogy that should be needed for Apache crews when confronting enemy combatants.

It's also good guidance for marine snipers. Unfortunately, they often receive other guidance. In April 2004, an Iraqi military-aged male in Fallujah who was scurrying around while carrying an AK-47 or rocket-propelled grenade (RPG) should have been targeted. Instead, a JAG, with commander concurrence, wrote ROE stating that the marines could not fire unless fired upon—not just threatened with a weapon, but actually fired on! Taking up this lawyer-imposed rallying cry, the 1st Armored Division mirrored this ROE. As Pogo said, "We have met the enemy and it is us!"

A clear example of how such hesitant and legally unnecessary thinking can disaffect the mission is the mindset of one of the army's snipers when confronted with a vehicle speeding toward a checkpoint he was manning. When asked what his initial mindset was when he had the motorist in his crosshair, Staff Sergeant Brandon House replied, "I hope I'm not going to be in trouble." Something is terribly wrong when even our trained hunter-killers like Staff Sergeant House have such thoughts when confronted with an imminent threat of death or serious bodily injury.[40]

This risk-averse behavior is not confined to overseas combat operations. Let's examine the November 5, 2009, massacre at Fort Hood, perpetrated by the enemy double agent Major Nidal Hasan. First, it is worth taking note of the history of recent attacks by such enemies within as detailed by Barrett Tillman in the January 2010 edition of *Proceedings* magazine:

> In Kuwait in 2003, a Muslim army sergeant "fragged" 16 Soldiers, killing two.
>
> Federal agents in New Jersey in 2007 arrested six Muslim immigrants who were convicted of planning an attack on Fort Dix, based on knowledge gained from pizza deliveries.
>
> In June 2009, a Muslim convert shot two soldiers at a Little Rock, Arkansas, recruiting office, killing one.[41]

Yet none of these victims or potential victims was allowed to carry firearms for self-defense. Tillman goes on to note:

> A Fort Hood officer was quoted in an Internet circular: "I've been trained how to respond to gunfire, but with my own weapon. To have no weapon, I don't know how to explain what that felt like."

In a truly professional army, he wouldn't have to know how it felt.

The problem is administrative, not tactical. Any military is a controlling institution, often with a powerful mistrust of troops. Therefore, careerists seek to control circumstances that could affect their retirement and impose bureaucratic limits on potential solutions. The unimaginative among them—the huge majority—default to school solutions. At Fort Hood, the school solution is additional civilian contractor and military police patrols.

Apparently nobody at Fort Hood has broken out of the school solution box by allowing professional soldiers to carry weapons. Says a retired Army NCO, "They'll start strip-searching troops arriving on base before any of them carry guns."[42]

Tillman's article becomes more prescient in light of the July 2011 arrest of Naser Jason Abdo, a Muslim convert recently granted conscientious objector status by the army, who desired to mimic Hasan by inflicting mass casualties against his fellow soldiers at Fort Hood. Only Abdo's arrest, facilitated by an astute clerk at a local gun store, prevented untold further carnage.

For an organization whose self-appellation is "the Armed Forces of the United States" to possess the fear and antipathy toward firearms that is only rivaled by Disney films or The Brady Campaign to Prevent Gun Violence (formerly Handgun Control, Inc.) is dangerous. Not only is it dangerous for the reasons cited by Barrett Tillman, but it is also dangerous in terms of mission readiness and the ability to kill in combat. The army's knee-jerk reaction: Register guns on-post and make doubly sure no one is armed, the typical response one would expect of a large corporation seeking to avoid liability. It is, however, anathema to warriors. Hundreds of thousands of police officers walk around America every day armed with pistols in "condition one" (locked and loaded) status. These officers, with a minimum of training, enter hospitals, schools, churches, and even mosques without feeling it necessary to clear their weapons at a clearing barrel. Yet this clearing-barrel mentality is what our warriors go through in combat zones when they come in from outside the wire. Once back stateside, they are disarmed and treated like ticking time bombs. They deserve better. If the warriors at Fort Hood were allowed to carry weapons, they would have shot Major Hasan into the ground well before he inflicted death and injury to the degree he did.

As long as the military continues to encourage and promote risk-averse officers, there is more likelihood of allowing off-duty marijuana smoking than there is of allowing service members to carry weapons for defense of self and others. This is because most leaders—even many infantry officers—are not very skilled in the martial arts of close personal violence and gunfighting. Quite simply, they are not gun guys. They fear the primary tool in their soldiers' toolkits—the individual weapon—as a necessary evil that should only be handled or taken out of the box when on actual combat operations.

Over the past four decades a philosophical sea change has occurred concerning attitudes toward weapons and weapons systems. Two generations' worth of exposure to the media's vilification of firearms has turned America from a nation that respected and relied on firearms to one that views weapons as either intrinsically evil or, at best, instruments to be feared.

For an entity that calls itself "the Armed Forces," most service members—perhaps with the exception of the marines—never initially develop an intimate and close relationship with firearms. Often to the contrary, service members are taught to fear rather than become masters of their individual weapons. Such fearful attitudes are reinforced by first-time experiences at basic military training ranges. There, and often throughout their careers, service members are exposed to well-intentioned but misguided leaders who are too focused on "safety" rather than true familiarization and development of tactically useful foundational skill sets.

CHAPTER FOUR

Rules of Engagement

The belief that machines fight wars and people are of secondary importance was exemplified by technological solutions to the ongoing enemy evolutions in the war in Iraq and Afghanistan. The high priests of technology in the Pentagon and industry (and their wholly owned subsidiaries in the media and think tanks) even have the temerity to construct a precisely defined vision of a high-tech world in 2025 through the RMA. It justified the past obsession with "revolutionary" precision-guided weapons and all-seeing, all-knowing command and control systems. Today, these same systems have not been able to defeat a third world insurgency. Only thinking leaders and soldiers can do that.[43]

—Franklin C. Spinney

More so than at any time in our history, American soldiers, sailors, airmen, and marines are being placed into situations where they have to make split-second decisions on whether or not to use deadly force in defense of self and innocent others. Their decisions are often judged in the clear vision of 20-20 hindsight by government, political, and media entities that do not understand the tactical realities of a firefight.

Because our forces have been in near-continuous combat since 2001, America possesses for the first time since WWII a high percentage of the

51

military force that has experienced combat. We now have a new generation of warriors who have performed as well as those who fought in WWII, but we are impeding them with rules that were established before September 11 and post-incident analyses.[44]

While the military has taken tremendous strides to recognize the importance of realistic tactical training and weapons familiarity—such as the tactics techniques and procedures shared with the deployed force by the Army's Asymmetric Warfare Group's mobile training teams, as well as recent changes to Basic Military Training (BMT) instituted by the Army Training and Doctrine Command (TRADOC)—in many ways we are still behaving like a risk-averse, peacetime military when it comes to rules of engagement drafting, implementation, and training. More disturbing is the trend to equate the life of an American with that of a foreigner—something that no veteran of World War II would ever dream of doing. "The only good Jap is a dead Jap" may not be polite words at a Department of State tea party, but such sentiments are appropriate when engaged in a life or death struggle.

> The U.S. response to attacks on American citizens and interests becomes proportionate, leaving the enemy intact and ready to kill again; and the U.S. government goes to war not against peoples, groups, or countries, but against individuals like Milosevic, Saddam, bin Laden, and Qaddafi. This is the nuanced, international-ballet-of-politics approach to U.S. foreign policy. Since 1991 the men and women who practiced this sort of diplomacy have produced policies that have consistently yielded dead Americans, undefeated U.S. enemies, and new crops of foes for the United States. These individuals are the enemies of common sense and the security of Americans that David Brooks indentifies as "bourgeoisophobes."[45]

As recently exemplified by the experience of Marine Lance Corporal Justin L. Sharratt, who faced court-martial charges stemming from his decision to use deadly force in Haditha, Iraq, on November 19, 2005, American service members are increasingly thrust into situations where they must make use of deadly force decisions more analogous to domestic law enforcement confrontations than traditional force-on-force combat operations. Much discord and confusion remains as to the authority and ability to use deadly force. Much of this confusion is not based on the rules themselves—rules that are, for the most part, rather robust—but rather on how the rules are interpreted and communicated to the lowest echelons and how they are trained.

In Haditha, on November 19, 2005, Lance Corporal Sharratt—a veteran of combat operations in Fallujah—engaged four civilian-dressed military-aged males while conducting a house-to-house search just hours after his convoy was hit during a roadside improvised explosive device (IED) attack. The end result of an intense and sometimes improperly focused investigation was an exoneration of Lance Corporal Sharratt after a hearing conducted pursuant to Article 32b of the Uniform Code of Military Justice (UCMJ). The convening authority—then-Lieutenant General James Mattis, who now serves as Commander, U.S. Central Command (CENTCOM), wrote a two-page letter to Lance Corporal Sharratt dismissing the charges. The relevant portions of General Mattis' poignant dismissal letter are set forth as follows:

> The experience of combat is difficult to understand intellectually and very difficult to appreciate emotionally. One of our Nation's most articulate Supreme Court Justices, Oliver Wendell Holmes, Jr., served as an Infantryman during the Civil War and described war as an "incommunicable experience."[46] He has also noted elsewhere that "detached reflection cannot be demanded in the presence of an uplifted knife."[47]

While the charges against Sharratt were eventually dismissed, the reality is that service members are indeed being unnecessarily subjected to detached reflection in the presence of uplifted AK-47s. Could one imagine such an inquiry resulting from the actions of Easy Company from *Band of Brothers*? Even if our leadership insists on such practices, many of those responsible for training our forces precombat, as well as those investigating our warriors postcombat, fail to appreciate the dynamics of a tactical encounter as experienced in close quarters combat (CQC).[48] In fact, Major General Eldon Bargewell, one of the few general officers with considerable CQC experience,[49] recently commented that the events of Haditha were the result of placing marines trained and experienced in conducting traditional Military Operations in Urban Terrain (MOUT) tactics in a CQC environment. In other words, if you use blunt instruments for precision surgery, don't be surprised at the resulting trauma to the body.

In 2008, a U.S. Army brigade assigned to the 4th Infantry Division was charged with keeping the peace in east Baghdad, including the notorious Sadr City. While building a wall around portions of the protected area, a number of the brigade's soldiers were killed and wounded by enemy sniper fire coming from an abandoned building adjacent to the wall's construction site.[50] The brigade commander, a seasoned infantry officer, first attempted to attenuate the situation by employing counter-sniper fire to the suspected sniper hides. After a while, tired of missing the enemy sniper and suffering more casualties, this wise commander called in an AH-64 Apache helicopter strike. Six Hellfire missiles razed the abandoned building and quelled the dangerous and deadly sniper fire. You would think that at least a "hurrah" or "job well done" would be in order. But no, three weeks later, a brigade legal advisor assigned to the aviation brigade to which the Apaches were attached reviewed the gun tapes of the mission. Safely and in the cool comfort of her legal trailer inside the wire of a forward operating base, she declared the use of the Hellfires excessive force. The brigade commander and the Apache team endured a one-star led AR 15-6 investigation, which exonerated the brigade commander. End of story? Not yet: The Division Commander, perhaps wanting to protect his own career from future scrutiny, issued a letter of reprimand to the brigade commander despite the investigating officer's recommendation to the contrary.

A little earlier in the war, in response to increased incidents of IED-initiated attacks, a group of special operators came up with a brilliant tactic to kill the enemy. The tactic involved staging a fake IED attack, complete with artillery simulators, smoke and fire, and then setting up SEAL snipers to kill enemy insurgents who nearly always arrived to follow up IED attacks with a ground assault. The new operation was having tremendous results—bad guys getting stacked up like cordwood—until it came to a screeching halt when a Navy JAG, operating at a higher headquarters, said that the SEAL snipers where "killing people for simply conducting acts of civil disobedience!" The incredibly effective tactic was abandoned.

Another gem of an example of the law and reason gone awry is when an Apache squadron commander was investigated after his birds launched an attack on four enemy combatants they observed digging a roadside hole and placing an IED. This investigation was launched because of what an adjacent unit discovered while conducting site exploitation of the area after the attack. In addition to the bodies of the four insurgents and IED material, the unit discovered two children's bodies in the hole. The legal onus for the child deaths should be squarely pegged on the insurgent enemy for allowing kids to play in the hole near their nefarious activities; instead scrutiny fell on the attacking unit for their use of force. The U.S. consistently eats its own on matters such as this, as if the local population's hearts and minds will be won over because we conduct investigations and prosecute the good guys.

On October 13, 2006, in Afghanistan on the Pakistan border, two United States Special Forces soldiers, Master Sergeant Troy Anderson and Captain Dave Staffel, assigned to Special Forces Operational Detachment Alpha (ODA) 374, 3rd Battalion, 3rd Special Forces Group were on the hunt for Nawab Buntangyar, a terrorist on the kill-capture list.

Captain Staffel learned from informants that Buntangyar could be found in a home near the village of Ster Kalay, so he ordered a seven-man team to investigate the tip. Driving toward Ster Kalay in two government vans, the Americans called the Afghan national police and border patrol officers to assist them. Since Buntangyar had already been vetted as a target by American commanders as an enemy combatant who could be legally killed once he was positively identified, all the Special Forces team needed was to gain such positive identification in order to carry out their mission.

After the Afghan police called Buntangyar outside and twice asked him to identify himself, they signaled, using a prearranged hand gesture, to Sergeant Anderson, concealed with a rifle about a hundred yards away. From a vehicle a few hundred yards farther away, Captain Staffel radioed Sergeant Anderson, "If you have a clear shot, take it." Confirming the order, Sergeant Anderson fired once, killing terrorist Buntangyar.

So using the rules of engagement in force at the time, which very clearly authorized the killing of a designated hostile such as Buntangyar, the Special Forces sniper team took the shot and killed this known terrorist. You would imagine that some sort of commendation would flow down the chain of command to these two fine warriors. In this risk-averse COIN environment, however, upper levels of command become squeamish at the thought of Americans actually killing the enemy up close and personal. The Special Operations Force community could not believe it when criminal charges were filed against these fine Americans. Army Major General Frank Kearney, then Commander of Special Operations Command Central, said that the snipers should have captured Buntangyar instead of killing him. Kearney believed that the strategic doctrine of minimum force applied at the tactical level. Mercifully the charges were dropped after a preliminary hearing, but not before the command climate in that theater was damaged beyond repair.

Many senior commanders have no problem dropping Joint Direct Attack Munitions (JDAMs) or ordering Hellfire strikes from Predator drones on similar types of targets, but when warriors actually put boots on the ground and risk their lives to affect such a killing these same senior leaders become squeamish. Most senior leaders in today's army do not understand the tactical dynamics of deadly force encounters and have never actually had to kill someone up close and personal. They grew up in a Bosnia-Kosovo, Wesley Clark-run army where political correctness trumped being a steely-eyed killer. One can judge the importance a leader places on a topic by how he spends money. Many of today's leaders spend millions on golf courses and little or nothing on firing ranges.

American civilian contractors as well are now subject to prosecutions not based upon the law, but rather upon political expediency. Unfortunately, such expediency compels prosecutors to flagrantly ignore exculpatory evidence in seeking indictments before grand juries. The following example is from the Blackwater case stemming from the Nisur Square engagement of September 2007:

> The prosecutors withheld from the second grand jury substantial exculpatory evidence that had been presented to the first grand jury. For instance, Raven 23 team members Thomas Vargas, Jeremy Skinner, Daniel Childers and Edward Randall all testified before the first grand jury that the Raven 23 convoy responded to incoming fire. Vargas testified before the first grand jury that approximately "five seconds after we pulled into our positions, we started taking fire" and that he "could hear AK-47 fire" and "immediately saw two insurgents." Skinner likewise testified that he heard gunfire and saw "two distinct separate muzzle flashes"

fired by insurgents at the Raven 23 convoy. Childers testified that he heard incoming gunfire coming from his seven to eight o'clock position. And Randall testified that the Raven 23 convoy took fire from the south and southwest and that he saw a round impact the side of one of the vehicles. Although Malis acknowledged that this testimony corroborated the defendants' self-defense theory, none of this testimony was presented to the second grand jury. Indeed, Malis testified that he chose not to present the testimony of these witnesses to the second grand jury because the testimony indicated that the witnesses were "hostile" to the prosecution.[51] [internal citations omitted]

The court went on to express how especially disturbing such prosecutorial acts are in light of the fact that

> DOJ guidelines require prosecutors to present exculpatory evidence to the grand jury. United States Attorneys' Manual § 9-11.233 (stating that "[i]t is the policy of the Department of Justice ... that when a prosecutor conducting a grand jury inquiry is personally aware of substantial evidence that directly negates the guilt of a subject of the investigation, the prosecutor must present or otherwise disclose such evidence to the grand jury before seeking an indictment against such a person").[52]

Of course, the mainstream media, our insurgent enemies, and unfortunately many senior officers in our military had already convicted these defendants in the court of public opinion. Even after the dismissal of the case in U.S. District Court, Vice President Joe Biden still couldn't leave it alone. Expressing "personal regret" over the Nisur Square incident, he said the U.S. Justice Department would file its appeal against the court's decision the next week. "The United States is determined to hold to account anyone who commits crimes against Iraqi people," Mr. Biden added. "While we fully respect the independence and the integrity of the US judicial system, we were disappointed with the judge's decision to dismiss the indictment, which was based on the way some evidence had been acquired."[53] We preach rule of law to other countries all the time, but when it comes to applying the protection of the rule of law to our own, we fall short due to external pressures and self-induced misperceptions of the strategic landscape. Or worse yet, for purely political reasons.

While some folks, as our friend John C. Hall is fond of saying, are "simply uneducable," most of such opinion, investigations, and prosecutions flow from fundamental misunderstandings of the legal authorities and tactical dynamics of the fight. Soldiers and marines are consistently and wrongly instructed that they must have PID (positive identification) before killing the enemy. Not only is the term PID misleading, but it is a targeting term that has nothing to do with the application of force in self-defense or close-in combat settings where the enemy is performing an overt hostile act, like emplacing an IED.

Another case is worthy of comment. In September 2007, First Lieutenant Michael Behenna deployed to Iraq with the 101st Airborne (Air Assault) Division for his first combat tour. Behenna, a Ranger-qualified infantry officer, was assigned as a platoon leader with that vaunted army division. On April 21, 2008, his platoon was attacked by al Qaeda in Iraq (AQI) insurgents. The insurgents employed an improvised explosive device (IED) roadside bomb in their attack, resulting in the death of two of the platoon members and two Iraqi citizens and wounding two soldiers, Specialists Adam Kohlhaas and Steven Christofferson.

On May 5, 2008, suspected AQI member Ali Mansur was detained at his home for suspected involvement in the attack on Behenna's platoon. Eleven days later, Mansur was released by the military intelligence team initially charged with interrogating him. Lieutenant Behenna, who had lost two members of his platoon just weeks earlier, was ordered to transport Mansur back to his home. During the transport, Lieutenant Behenna futilely attempted a final interrogation of Mansur prior to his release. During the interrogation—and this is where the facts become fuzzy—Behenna is either forced to use deadly force in self-defense when attacked by Mansur or he simply executes Mansur. Either way: an AQI member dies.

In July 2008, the U.S. Army charged Lieutenant Behenna with premeditated murder for the death of al Qaeda operative and terrorist Ali Mansur. They also charged him with failing to report the incident, although who can blame him in light of the panicked reaction of so many senior officers over the use of force.

But the story doesn't end there. As in the ill-fated *Blackwater* case described above, the prosecutorial team was so bent on getting this politically correct conviction that they hid exculpatory evidence from the defense team and, ultimately, the jury (or panel as it is known in courts-martial settings). Here are the facts:

- February 23, 2009: The *U.S. v. Behenna* trial begins at Fort Campbell, Kentucky. Behenna raises the affirmative defense of self-defense, alleging that Mansur lunged in an attempt at disarming his captors.
- Government and defense experts agreed on the trajectory of the bullets killing Mansur. The only question was whether Mansur was sitting or standing.
- A prosecution expert, Dr. Herbert L. MacDonnell, after observing Lieutenant Behenna testify about the facts surrounding the shooting, said to the three prosecutors, "The explanation that Lieutenant Behenna just testified to was the exact same scenario I told you yesterday. Lieutenant Behenna is telling the truth."
- Specifically, Dr. MacDonnell told army prosecutor Captain Meghan M. Poirier that he had changed his mind and now believed that Behenna killed Ali Mansur in self-defense. In a letter dated February 27, 2009, Dr. MacDonnell told Poirier he was "concerned that I did not testify and have a chance to inform the court of the only logical explanation for this shooting."

  "From the evidence I feel that Ali Mansur had to have been shot in his chest when he was standing. As he dropped straight down he was shot again at the very instant that his head passed in front of the muzzle," Dr. MacDonnell wrote. "It fits the facts and I cannot think of a more logical explanation."
- The prosecution team did not call Dr. MacDonnell to testify in the case, and he was instead sent home. Jack Zimmermann, one of Lieutenant Behenna's defense counsel, asked the prosecutors if they had any exculpatory evidence that should be provided to the defense, and specifically referred to Dr. MacDonnell's demonstration. The army prosecutors denied having any such evidence, despite having a legal duty to reveal to the defense such "exculpatory evidence" that could clear Behenna.
- The prosecution's withholding of this evidence allowed them to argue in closing arguments Lieutenant Behenna executed Ali Mansur while he was seated despite the fact that their own forensic expert

agreed that Mansur was standing with his arms outstretched when he was shot by Lieutenant Behenna.

- Behenna is subsequently convicted of unpremeditated murder and assault by a military panel of seven officers, none of whom had combat experience.
- Dr. MacDonnell contacts the prosecution requesting that the information provided in his demonstration be given to the defense. The prosecutors provided the information only after a verdict was rendered.
- On March 20, 2009, Army First Lieutenant Michael Behenna was sentenced to twenty-five years in prison for killing Ali Mansur, a known al Qaeda terrorist cell member: a group declared hostile under the theater rule of engagement.
- On March 20, the military judge denied a defense motion to declare a mistrial and to order a new trial based on the recently divulged exculpatory information.

Mistake one: Ali Mansur, by joining and aiding AQI, should have been targeted and killed by U.S. forces. Instead, he is treated like a criminal suspect by our military intelligence forces. Mistake two: The army assigned the platoon leader of a platoon that just suffered deaths and injuries due to AQI's nefarious activities as the escort officer to release this thug. Mistake three: The army did not stand by its own and assess the matter under the law of self-defense. It did not heed Winston Churchill's caution and so remained "neutral between the fire and the fire brigade." Mistake four: The army achieved a conviction built upon prosecutorial misconduct. We improperly sent a warrior to jail for killing a member of AQI. Mistake five: The army only focuses Law of War investigations and prosecutions on its own.

Speaking directly to our warriors out there who may be the subject or target of a use of force investigation: Do not be intimidated by AR 15-6 investigators or anyone else. If you use deadly force in the line of duty, follow these guidelines.

1. Avail yourself of switched-on counsel *before* making a statement, especially a sworn statement. The right to counsel is not only for criminals: It is a right guaranteed for all Americans. It is perfectly

reasonable to provide a quick Situational Report (Sit Rep) to your chain of command. They have a need to know enemy tactics and a need to provide higher headquarters with situational awareness on the incident. It is not reasonable, however, to question and obtain sworn statements from a soldier at two in the morning thirty minutes post-incident. There are a number of reasons why this is true. Suppose at an entry control point (ECP) to a sensitive facility a soldier uses deadly force on a bulkily clad civilian-dressed female who fails to heed repeated warnings to halt. In a personal-borne improvised explosive device (PBIED) suicide bomber environment, such force may be perfectly reasonable. Suppose, however, that post-incident it is discovered that the bulkily clad civilian was merely a disoriented pregnant female seeking medical attention. A soldier, feeling guilty for an otherwise lawful use of force, may make self-incriminating, factually incorrect statements. The human mind, after a deadly force encounter, is often encumbered with intrusive thoughts, elation, guilt, and multiple compressed, inaccurate memories. For these reasons alone, it is provident to wait at least twenty-four hours before making a statement.

2. Understand the preassaultive behaviors of the enemy and be prepared to articulate them. A switched-on attorney can help articulate these in a sworn statement.

3. Do not succumb to the arguments of investigators that if you don't have anything to hide, why not make a statement? This is a bullying tactic that should be saved for criminals, not warriors. Moreover, if the law gives such a privilege as the right to remain silent to criminals, it certainly owes the same deference to the fine Americans making life-or-death decisions in the line of duty. And in the end, so long as one acts reasonably, all will end well. The law, for the foreseeable future, is on your side. Interestingly enough, by policy, federal law enforcement agencies will not allow their agents who are involved in line-of-duty shootings to make a statement for at least twenty-four hours post-incident, and then only after the agent has had an opportunity to decompress and speak with counsel, psychologist, or chaplain if he chooses. We should provide the same courtesies to warriors who make decisions in situations that are often more tense and dangerous than those facing law enforcement.

There aren't enough signs that these same courtesies are being extended. Disturbingly, the military will occasionally whipsaw its subordinate commanders with mixed messages as reported by the *Washington Post*'s Greg Jaffe:

> The U.S. military has reprimanded an unusually large number of commanders for battlefield failures in Afghanistan in recent weeks, reflecting a new push by the top brass to hold commanders responsible for major incidents in which troops are killed or wounded, said senior military officials . . . The reprimands come amid growing political pressure from lawmakers who have pushed the military to assign greater accountability for incidents in which large numbers of U.S. troops are killed or wounded.[54]

The irony of this reaction is astounding. The reprimanded subordinate commanders' reluctance to engage the enemy directly stems from the inordinate pressures not to engage the enemy previously emanating from the same higher headquarters now issuing these reprimands! Countless directives and targeting restrictions imposed by higher headquarters have created an enduring hesitancy to fire artillery rounds or provide aviation close air support even in response to calls for help from troops in contact with the enemy. This hesitation to provide reasonable and necessary force in response to fellow Americans' desperate calls for help is directly attributable to a fear of being investigated and reprimanded for causing "unnecessary civilian deaths."

Countless directives not to fire anywhere near civilian-populated areas, even when the *muj* fire on Americans from those areas, are the result of profound misunderstandings of both the Law of War and the history of warfare itself. Again our senior leaders make the mistake of assigning a moral equivalency between *muj* and American lives. When they are called on the carpet for this error, instead of acknowledging the mistake and taking corrective action, the senior leaders simply blame their subordinates for what are otherwise their own failures. No one is holding senior military and civilian leaders accountable for their cowardly derelictions of duty. Sadly our warriors are paying the tab with their careers and sometimes their lives.

An aviation battalion commander who recently returned from Iraq explained this dilemma in very personal and real terms:

> I was out flying one day and responded to a call for a QRF [Quick Response Force]. I flew to the site of a roadside IED event, where the insurgents struck one of our Bradleys. Upon arriving at the scene I observed three American bodies slumped out of the top of the still-smoldering Bradley. No insurgents were in sight, so it was a very frustrating experience.
>
> Later that evening, one of my lieutenants came in to see me. He wanted to thank me for allowing him to fly home to the United States as escort for one of the victims of the IED attack: his brother.
>
> I immediately walked around my desk, embraced this fine young officer, and promised him I would do all I could to kill those responsible and those like them.
>
> The next night, I personally went out on an extended night mission looking for IED emplacers. After about the fifth hour of flying with night vision goggles, with ghost images fried into my eyes, I spied a civilian-dressed insurgent carrying explosives from the trunk of a vehicle to a roadside emplacement. I immediately got on the net and requested clearance to fire—not for permission, but only to ensure there were not friendlies in the area. As soon as the clearance came back, I sent a Hellfire up that guy's ass, and it felt good. I sure as hell went out with the idea of killing someone on my mind, and it was the right thing to do!

This battalion commander instinctively and rightly knew the difference between the value of his men's lives and the insurgents' lives. King Leonidas of Sparta would get it; a World War II marine would get it; and most Americans would get it. Yet one is left to wonder if our strategic leaders, so enamored with their COIN doctrine and "minimum uses of force" moral equivalency, would get it.

This slide toward moral equivalency makes no sense to a warrior. If all civilizations and cultures are morally equivalent, which one is worth fighting and dying for? Can you imagine the leaders of the Spartans at Thermopylae, the British soldiers in Wellington's square at Waterloo, or even

our marines at Iwo Jima telling their subordinates to use minimum force if
attacked? Yet this is happening so often now it runs the risk of becoming
entrenched doctrine. When fed this line, no subordinate commander dares
to question its efficacy or rationale: After all, it was our leaders who developed the doctrine. Those, like Mike Steele, who do question it by action
are marginalized. At our senior service schools, instead of questioning the
doctrine, we line up two-by-two to develop even more complex and
VUCA-like analyses and solutions.

A recent example concerning rules of engagement and how we use
force in combat is set forth in the following news item from May 4, 2010:

> U.S. and NATO troops in Afghanistan could someday be awarded
> medals for restraint that prevents civilian casualties in combat.
>
> The possibility is under consideration by the staff of Gen.
> Stanley McChrystal, the commander in Afghanistan, according to
> Lt. Col. Tadd Sholtis, McChrystal's spokesman.
>
> The idea of rewarding battlefield restraint was proposed by
> British Maj. Gen. Nick Carter, who is in charge of the interna-
> tional forces in southern Afghanistan. Sholtis said the idea is still
> in its "conceptual stage."
>
> "Although no decisions have been made on the award itself,
> the idea is consistent with our strategic approach," Sholtis said.
> "Our young men and women display remarkable courage every
> day, including situations where they refrain from using lethal
> force, even at risk to themselves, in order to prevent possible
> harm to civilians. In some situations our forces face in
> Afghanistan, that restraint is an act of discipline and courage not
> much different than those combat actions that merit awards for
> valor."[55]

Perhaps the biggest affront to reason and the law is this singular focus
of the military legal system on the behavior of our forces to the complete
and utter disregard of the behavior of the enemy. If an enemy openly violates the Law of War—like using civilians as shields, blowing up civilian
schools and marketplaces, and using every known method of perfidy, to
include the use of poison chlorine gas—why are we not prosecuting them
in military tribunals as we did the Nazis after World War II? Instead many

judge advocates and commanders perpetuate the "blame America" mentality by judging the combat actions of its own forces after the fact from the position of safety. Meanwhile, Attorney General Eric Holder fights for the rights of our enemies.

The threats to America, as well as the integrity and strength of our military, require a much more rigorous and honest analysis. If warriors and the American public don't push back against this trend toward the greening of our military, our Western civilization runs the risk of being overwhelmed by determined enemies unburdened by hesitancy or lack of a clear objective.

Much of this could be remedied from the top by rewriting Standing Rules of Engagement (SROE) to more clearly set forth the inherent individual right of self-defense and training our forces to this standard. A proposed rewrite is set forth in the concluding chapter.

CHAPTER FIVE

Right of Sovereignty

The increasing tendency of the West to ignore the right of sovereignty of nations is disturbing both in its flouting of international law and for the unintended consequences such courses of action create. The United States' use of force, either unilaterally or in alliance with others, has historically been predicated on self-defense. Deliberate consideration for the sovereign rights of other nations, without regard to their internal governance, has always been the hallmark of our intercourse with foreign nations. Rarely have we deviated from such policy:

> The creation of a major supply route to Russia through the Persian Gulf became our prime objective . . . Starting in September 1941, this enterprise, begun and developed by the British Army, and presently to be adopted and expanded by the United States, enabled us to send to Russia, over a period of four and a half years, five million tons of supplies. Thus ended a brief and fruitful exercise of overwhelming force against a weak and ancient state. Britain and Russia were fighting for their lives. *Inter arma silent leges.*[56]

Thus, Winston Churchill explained his divergence from the otherwise sound policy of respecting the sovereignty of nations. Unless our national interests are threatened, the United States should refrain from interfering in the internal affairs of sovereign nations. To liberal internationalists, however, the concept of minding one's own business is anathema.

The United States' national interest comes first, before the collective goals of the international community. Self-defense—individual, collective, or anticipatory—must be the cause of any use of force, and not the attempt to impose our will on the internal functions of a sovereign state. Guided by this principle, America should gauge the use of military force to reach its enduring goals of security, prosperity, and preservation of American values rooted in our Constitution.

Clearly stated, both our adversaries and our allies will know our intent and resolve. And the result will be a more secure world marketplace for commerce, ideas, and freedom.

National Interest

It is only when fighting for our national interest, as recognized by the people, that America can sustain the will to fight. This simple truth was recognized over 2,500 years ago by Sun Tzu, who observed that national unity was an essential requirement of victorious war.[57] Many in the European Union (EU) and the United Nations (UN) derisively refer to America as a nation of cowboys.[58] America's economic and social strengths derive from precisely the fact that we are not a parliamentary European Union-like entity, but rather a free market society unafraid of being a cowboy. But, like a good cowboy, we should only use force in self-defense.

Unfortunately America has ceded its core values and security to a conglomerate of diverse, international interests, diminishing its power and sovereignty to the point of becoming a second-tier voice in a parliamentary aggregate slouching toward socialistic mediocrity. As Sir Winston Churchill stated, "The greatest vice of capitalism is the unequal sharing of blessings, while the greatest virtue of socialism is the equal sharing of miseries."[59] As such, America's economic engine must run on the fuel of free market economics, respect and integrity of private property rights and state sovereignty, and security from external threats. Threats to the United States today and into the foreseeable future recognize that America's center of gravity is the strength of our free market economy and our republican form of limited government. The primacy of these national interests as the foundation of our societal will to fight must be protected rather than squandered in fields afar for nebulous purposes such as nation-building or that Johnny-come-lately liberal notion of Responsibility to Protect, or R2P.

In essence, R2P advocates claim that if a sovereign nation loses the ability to maintain internal governance and cannot protect civilians from internal abuses, then that responsibility must be transferred to the international community. In a right thinking world, if a de jure state lost its de facto ability to govern, then it was replaced either by internal revolution or coup or by external absorption by a neighboring power. Now the globalists or internationalists want to solve all world problems via "peaceful" means. Unfortunately, their peaceful means often involve the coercive use of American military force.

Of particular note is the penchant of R2P advocates and those similarly pushing for an enhanced military capability for stability operations as their focus for keeping the coercive power solely within the state. In other words, these people are usually the ones that so stridently want to disarm the population. In a weird twist, this penchant flies in the face of a true COIN warrior's advice on this matter. U.S. Army Brigadier General Sean McFarland, commenting on lessons he learned when he was a brigade commander in Iraq's al Anbar province in 2006 and 2007, stated:

> The people are indeed the key to the solution. It is not enough to protect the population; they must be given the means to protect themselves. Bottom line: We promised them the means to secure themselves in a way that did not disrupt their cultural order.[60]

But, it must be realized, affording the individual with the right to protect himself does not concern R2P advocates. Rather, R2P dangerously expands the self-possessed authority of the United Nations and other world bodies to violate the sovereignty of nations. As exemplified by modern theorists and legal scholars,[61] many are stridently pushing America to the brink of subservience to the United Nations or some similar supernumerary. While such international organizations have utility in reaching accords concerning aviation, laws of the sea, and similar treaties and agreements relating to free trade and commerce, they should never reach a level of primacy over America's core constitutional principles. "Do not let spacious plans for a new world divert your energies from saving what is left of the old," as Winston Churchill put it.[62] The lawful authority, both domestic and international, for the United States to use force is most emphatically rooted in the right of self-defense. By keeping all uses of military power—specifically war and warlike actions—founded in self-defense, America will retain the moral high ground, clearly signal its strategic intentions to potential adversaries, and avoid straying into the morass of commitments with unforeseen second- and third-order effects such as endless nation-building efforts and increased enmity of many in the Third World.

Even under international constructs, it should be noted that customary and statutory international law recognizes the inherent right of self-defense. The application of anticipatory or preemptive self-defense and the maxim of a person's inherent right to self-defense were firmly established in the *Caroline* incident. In 1837, the British were fighting a counterinsurgency war along the Niagara River in Canada. The steamer *Caroline* was being used by the insurgents on both the American and British sides of the river. On the evening of December 29, 1837, British combatants crossed onto the American side of the river and destroyed the *Caroline* while it was docked in Schlosser, New York. The Americans protested, but the British responded that they were merely exercising their inherent right of self-defense. American Secretary of State Daniel Webster disagreed. In response to Lord Ashburton's claim that the British acted in self-defense, Webster declared that for an act to be self-defense, it "must be a necessity of self-defense, instant, overwhelming, leaving no choice of means and no moment for deliberation." Secondly, to be appropriate, self-defense must be proportional, not "unreasonable or excessive."[63] While never admitting culpability for the *Caroline* incident, the British apologized to the United States for the incident. The *Caroline* incident is the first recognition of the common law right of self-defense as it relates to international law.[64] Lieutenant Commander Dale Stephens wrote:

> The *"Caroline"* correspondence indicates, however, that the authors themselves drew upon natural law concepts and combined them with municipal notions of self defense as then understood in Anglo-American criminal law. In this regard, the authors were acknowledging the personal and instinctive nature of self defense. Lord Ashburton plainly stated in his response to Mr. Webster of 28 July 1842, that self defense "is the first law of our

nature, and it must be recognized by every code which professes to regulate the conditions and relations of man." Further, Lord Ashburton was plainly aware of the novel nature of the American proposition that international actions may be justified by a combination of the established principle of necessity and the national legal concept of self defense. Lord Ashburton specifically noted the "ingenious" suggestion by Mr. Webster that the legitimacy of British actions should be assessed by reference to this modified concept of self defense under international law. Thus, the British suddenly found themselves defending their Captain's actions on the basis of a principle narrower than self-preservation. Further, Lord Ashburton accepted the challenge and consistently described his justification of British actions in terms analogous to personal self defense.

In 1928, Secretary of State Frank Kellogg, author of the Kellogg-Brian Pact (also known as the Pact of Paris), said: "The right of self defense is inherent in every sovereign state and is implicit in every treaty. Every nation is free at all times and regardless of treaty provisions to defend its territory from attack or invasion and it alone is competent to decide whether circumstances require recourse to war in self defense."[65] The Pact of Paris renounced war as a mechanism to resolve international disputes, and later served as the basis for the charge of crimes against peace prosecuted against Nazi war criminals at the Nuremberg International Military Tribunal following World War II. Kellogg recognized that a sovereign nation, by means of its individuals, has an inherent right to defend itself from outside aggressions, and that right was neither created by, nor can be abrogated by, written international law or treaty.

The International Military Tribunal reaffirmed Daniel Webster's definition of self-defense when ruling that the German invasion of Norway in 1940 was not defensive because it was unnecessary to prevent an imminent Allied invasion. The tribunal echoed Webster's criteria for self-defense, stating: "preventative action in foreign territory is justified only in case of an instant and overwhelming necessity for self-defense, leaving no choice of means, and no moment of deliberation."[66]

Lastly, in this vein, if America limits itself to only using force in self-defense, it will retain the steadfast approval of the vast majority of its public behind any war effort. Such general and sustained approval has been lacking since World War II. War itself is too full of chance and uncertainty to embark upon without such strong public support. Winston Churchill understood this when he said:

> Never, never, never believe any war will be smooth and easy, or that anyone who embarks on the strange voyage can measure the tides and hurricanes he will encounter. The statesman who yields to war fever must realise that once the signal is given, he is no longer the master of policy but the slave of unforeseeable and uncontrollable events.[67]

For two decades now, and somewhat in earnest since 2001, America has been involved in a war on terror. Yet we suffer from so many spasmodic divergences—nation-building, stability operations, and outright incursions into the sovereign territory of otherwise contained and benign nations—that we have lost our bearing, direction, and the support of the American people. This is not a sound theory of war or grand strategy.

Bill Clinton wagged his finger and promised to the American public that we would give the Balkans "one year . . . one year to show results and then we bring the troops home."[68] Troops are still in the Balkans.

Kosovo

Some from the Clinton administration point to the United States' intervention in Kosovo as a moral victory and an example of a successful multinational operation. Interestingly it is often these same liberal internationalists who want to use the military to achieve their goals. Madeleine Albright's 1993 statement to Colin Powell—"What's the point of having this superb military that you're always talking about if we can't use it?"—comes to mind. What these folks fail to say is that such an intervention violated all of Serbia's rights of sovereignty under international law. Serbia was involved in a messy, bloody civil war and was dealing with a violent and aggressive Muslim-based insurgency in its Kosovo province. Serbia's methods in dealing with the insurgency were violent and barbaric. Violence and barbarism, however, were extant on both sides of the internal conflict. But Serbia presented no threat to the territorial integrity of sur-rounding nations and certainly no threat to the United States. The Clinton administration knew that American citizens would not tolerate risking their sons and daughters in a ground war to support such a cause. Hence, Clinton ordered the clean, painless, surgical air strikes into Belgrade.

Clean, painless, and surgical only to those watching from the safety of an air operations center hundreds of miles away or from the comfort of their living rooms back in the States. The betrayal and pain felt by the Serbs on the ground (and, collaterally, Russia) was nearly incomprehensible. Was not Kosovo the site of the historic battleground where Serbs fought heroically to stem the Muslim tide in 1389? (The Battle of Kosovo was fought on St. Vitus' Day, June 15, 1389, between Serbian forces and the Ottoman Empire, in the Kosovo Field five kilometers northwest of modern-day Pristina.) The unintended consequences of the NATO-led air campaign against and subsequent occupation of Kosovo are still felt today. It feeds Russian concerns over the expansion of NATO. Moreover, it belies the claim that NATO is a defensive entity.

Serbian President Slobodan Milošević faced severe acts of rebellion and lawlessness conducted and supported by the Kosovo Liberation Army (KLA). The KLA received financial and material support from the Kosovo Albanian Diaspora and many Muslim-based external groups. The Yugoslavian Serb government clearly saw the KLA as a terrorist organization. In fact, in 1998, the U.S. State Department listed the KLA as a terrorist organization. There was even evidence that the KLA was involved in Albanian criminal syndicates and elements of radical Islam receiving support from Iran and al Qaeda. Yet in 1999 the United States sought to form a relationship with the KLA.[69] This relationship blossomed into a full-fledged air and ground campaign.

The air campaign itself, conducted between March 24 and June 10, 1999, was a U.S.-led bombing of Serbian Yugoslavia in an effort to force Milošević to withdraw from Kosovo. Ironically this military action was not authorized by the United Nations Security Council. It was a clear violation of international law and contrary to the provisions of the United Nations Charter. Despite this inconvenient truth, the United States recognized Kosovo as an independent state in 2008.

To put such an operation into perspective, consider the American Civil War as a distant mirror. Had Great Britain or France in 1864, in an effort to

stop the bloodshed and carnage, entered militarily into the sovereign territory of the United States? The carnage extant on American soil at the time
far outpaced the death and destruction in the Serbian civil war of 1998.
Was not Sherman's march on Georgia an act of violence against a civilian
populace designed to quell rebellion and lawlessness? Thank God that
NATO was not around in 1864!

And other than in Kosovo or Albania, did the United States' efforts in
taking the Muslim side in this civil war gain us respect in the Muslim
world at large? No! Treble that for Europe, where its Muslim indigenous
population continues to display Western-style "tolerance" for free speech
as witnessed by the violent rioting that broke out in Europe in 2005 after
the Mohammed "Bomb Head" cartoons were posted in a Danish newspa-
per. The cartoonist, Kurt Westergaard, depicted Prophet Mohammed with a
bomb in his turban and has been under police protection since his carica-
tures of the Prophet led to death threats. This, however, did not stop a January 2010 attack at Westergaard's home in Denmark by a Somali man
armed with an axe and suspected of links with al Qaeda. Denmark's Security and Intelligence Service (PET), a department of the national police,
said in a statement: "It is PET's impression that the attempted assassination
of the cartoonist Kurt Westergaard is terror related." Interestingly there was
no such statement here in the United States from either the FBI or our
intelligence agencies that Major Hasan's murderous attack at Fort Hood
was terror related, despite the fact that Hasan was screaming "Allahu
Akbar" while carrying out the attack.

Iraq

For all of us sitting poised to attack Iraq in late March 2003, the mission
was fairly straightforward: A change of regime and elimination of weapons
of mass destruction. Whether one now flyspecks the intelligence reports
and disputes their estimates in the clear vision of hindsight or not, that was
our mission. Assuming the intelligence reports were true, and no one
believed otherwise at the time, the United States' attack on Iraq in March
2003 was a legally defensible act of preemptive self-defense.

Nowhere was the concept of nation-building or setting up a democratically based rule of law set forth as a reason for entering the sovereign

territory of Iraq. It was, as many have written since, never seriously con-templated by our national leadership. In fact, when the military planners at CENTCOM floated estimates of what was needed for Phase IV (the stabi-lization phase of the operation), they were bluntly told to butt out by Rumsfeld and others. The Department of State and other government agen-cies would take the lead for that effort. History has clearly shown what a pipedream that estimate was, and many, like Tom Ricks and Bob Wood-ward, have written about it in detail.

But, in Rumsfeld's favor, the military should not have taken the lead in Phase IV: nation-building should be reserved to the Department of State, · its Agency for International Development (USAID), and diverse non-governmental organizations (NGOs). The military is designed to break things and kill people, not ensure governance beyond the initial stages of martial law necessary to preserve public order. One problem with Rums-feld's approach was his desire to stick around and nation-build without considering the second- and third-order effects of disenfranchising the Baathists and micromanaging Iraq's attempts at self-governance with the proverbial ten-thousand-mile screwdriver. Sometime during the critical 2003–2004 timeframe, when there was still a chance for a quick hand-off of control to the Iraqis, some policy advisors determined that former Baath party members should neither participate nor be employed by the new gov-ernment. This order had the effect of disenfranchising tens of thousands of people, many with martial skills in a violent environment. Showing an unbelievable ignorance of our battle space, this diplomat was willfully ignorant or, worse, criminally negligent in his duties of assessing the impact of his actions. When Saddam Hussein ran the Baathist party, it con-trolled everything within the country of Iraq. If you needed a house—you better be a Baathist. If you were an officer in the military—you became a Baathist. To have upward mobility within Iraqi society you needed to be a Baathist. The end result was that the talent, leadership, and management experience throughout the country of Iraq was all Baathist, if in name only. The ruling to exclude former Baathists from any role in the security and control of the new Iraq was ill-advised, and we paid dearly. We also did not learn from history. The American and British occupiers of Germany after World War II wisely ignored orders to de-Nazify the local governance.

Naturally, in Iraq, the military was left holding the hot potato in all of this. Doing what it often does best, improvising and approaching problems with a "git 'er done" mentality, the military became mired in a quasi-civil war and COIN fight.

Now, almost four years after the surge in Iraq, the U.S. military has proven its ability and resolve to "git 'er done," but that reflects the courage, stamina, and strength of our force rather than the propriety and efficacy of using the military in such a fashion. And as a result of the military's successes in Iraq, the COIN doctrine so effectively crafted and instilled by General David Petraeus and his staff runs the risk of becoming America's grand strategy in Afghanistan and future operations. It drives not only the budget process through the Quadrennial Defense Review (QDR), but also how the art of war is taught through every level of our warriors' military education.

The QDR is a legislatively mandated review of Department of Defense strategy and priorities. It also helps shape the long-term course for the military. Further, the QDR is supposed to assess threats and challenges and refocus the department's strategies, capabilities, and forces. The review is also intended to tie together the long-term national security landscape with plans for forces, equipment, and budgets. The latest QDR, released in February 2010, is a masterpiece of VUCA-speak, but fails to clearly identify the threats or concrete military roles. Instead it moves us away from defensive postures that would prepare our forces to fight and win wars to murky, globalized statements that transform our military into a ponderous intelligence, law enforcement, peacekeeping, and nation-building entity. One day, we will all be wearing Star Trek uniforms and have our phasers set on "stun" rather than "kill."

CHAPTER SIX

Become a Jeffersonian Democracy or Else

We are building a country that follows the rule of law" is a recurring theme among those fomenting for increased use of the military in America's global quests. While it sounds reasonable, it ignores an important underlying principle: the rule of law is not what is to be served; rather the rule of law must serve a social contract of a higher order. By way of example, the citizens of Germany were following "the rule of law" when Hitler ordered the confiscation of privately owned firearms in 1934 or the classification of Jewry under the Nürnberg Laws. Therefore, you must first be able to recognize that there are degrees of righteousness of principle, and it is important to properly discriminate among the world's diverse theories of governance. Unfortunately, many of the people clamoring for a global rule of law fail to distinguish this point and are willing to cede our tried-and-true superior form of constitutional governance.

Imagine if the United States, due to a massive catastrophic act of God or as the result of a deliberate terror attack that crippled its economy to the point of anarchy, was unable to control violence within its borders. Then imagine if the United Nations sent peacekeepers and nation-building forces into our sovereign territory to establish a rule of law. And never mind that the rule of law that the UN wished to impose is contrary to our traditions, culture, and Constitution. How would the average American respond? You would suspect that there would be a huge and hopefully successful insurgency to fight off the blue-helmeted scoundrels. Yet our current crop of strategic thinkers consistently ignores this reality in other countries and cultures. Moreover we have developed an entire Field Manual—Stability Operations—in what amounts to a noble but doomed attempt to provide commanders and other army personnel with a guide for supporting broader U.S. government efforts to deliver development, reconstruction, and humanitarian aid in war-torn nations. This plan is nothing short of a recipe for increasing the influence of the military over our other elements of national power: diplomatic, information, and economic.

Army officials described the document as a roadmap from conflict to peace. "Our objective, when we go into a foreign country, is to leave but to leave with that country safe and secure," said Lieutenant General William Caldwell, then commander of the U.S. Army Combined Arms Center. "If we work to ensure stability has returned, it will allow their people to live their lives in an orderly manner, feeling safe and secure."[70]

The coercive and constructive capabilities of military force, the manual says, can establish security; facilitate reconciliation between adversaries; establish political, legal, social, and economic institutions; and ultimately transition responsibility to a civil authority. The odds for success are slim.

The manual mirrors a U.S. defense strategy released in July 2008 that says military operations should play a supporting role for soft power initiatives to undermine militancy by promoting economic, political, and social development in vulnerable corners of the world. Let's undermine the militants' claims that Western Crusaders are attempting to subvert Islam by establishing a Western-style and -led constabulary force within their traditional and sacred Muslim lands. "The greatest threats to our national security will not come from emerging ambitious states but from nations unable or unwilling to meet the basic needs and aspirations of their people," the new army manual states. Tell that to China, Russia, India, and a nuclear-armed Iran.

America can serve as a model for emerging nation states, but only by their choosing and not our coercion. America's strength lies with its constitutionally guaranteed pact with its citizens: the government will serve the people only to the extent that it preserves the individual freedoms for the people to excel and prosper. The growth and prosperity of the United States under its constitutional republican form of government has served as a beacon of hope for generations of immigrants who have come to America to join in this form of government.

Attempts to export such notions to races of people that are fundamentally unaccustomed and ill-suited to a constitutional republic are foolish and arrogant. Such attempts are not only doomed to failure, but they will also serve as the catalyst for generating extreme anti-American hatred and sentiment among those peoples. Yet such efforts continue at full throttle. Consider this January 28, 2010, communiqué from the United Kingdom:

> The London Conference will be followed by a conference in Kabul later this year, hosted by the Afghan Government, where it intends to take forward its programme with concrete plans for delivery for the Afghan people. These should be based on democratic accountability, equality, human rights, gender equality, good governance and more effective provision of government services, economic growth, as well as a common desire to live in peace under the Afghan Constitution. We remain convinced that together we will succeed.[71]

Never mind that "democratic accountability, equality, human rights, gender equality, good governance and . . . a desire to live in peace" have never been the hallmarks of the tribal governments of Afghanistan. And, again, what business is it of outside nations to try to force these people, at gunpoint, to such a state?

In the mid-1990s the United States established fairly good bilateral relations with the Afghan-Taliban government, with a view toward limiting the areas for potential terrorist camps. This last point is what is supposedly at the center of our national interest there now. A group of feminists in America, led by Jay Leno's wife, took exception to how women were treated in Afghanistan, and pressure from these feminists' groups led to the break off of bilateral talks with Afghanistan. We consistently fail to appreciate the second- and third-order effects of such myopic policy decisions. No matter the blood, sweat, and toil we till into the plains of Afghanistan, that region will never become a liberal democracy. Our attempts to create one there will only result in the further radicalization of thousands of Muslims. As Major Jim Gant, U.S. Army Special Forces, explains, "Afghan tribes always have and always will resist any type of foreign intervention in their affairs. This includes a central government located in Kabul, which to them is a million miles away from their problems, a million miles away from their security."[72]

Moreover, what business is it of the United States to try and impose our values by coercion there or anywhere else? It is like the anti-Apartheid pressures of the 1980s leveraged against the sovereign Republics of South Africa and Rhodesia. Hindsight, except to the most myopic liberal, has shown how well that has boded for the region: Two countries that were the only semblance of economic strength and stability in an otherwise sub-Saharan Marxist sinkhole are now sliding toward failed-state status . . . but the liberals still feel good and Dave Matthews can brag at concerts that he got to smoke dope with Nelson Mandela, bragging witnessed in person by one of the authors in May 1996 after being dragged by friends to a Dave Matthews concert in Richmond, Virginia. It was the last such concert he has attended.

If the United States attempts to influence other nations and spread the rule of law and democracy, it should do so subtly and with elements of power other than the military. Using the military will only result in claims of hegemony and the concurrent diminished capability of the military to wage hard, violent, and effective war when necessary.

CHAPTER SEVEN

Our Risk-Averse Senior Officer Corps

The views of subordinates and peers play no role in an officer's advancement; to move up he must only please his superiors. In a system in which senior officers select for promotion those like themselves, there are powerful incentives for conformity. It is unreasonable to expect that an officer who spends 25 years conforming to institutional expectations will emerge as an innovator in his late forties . . . As matters stand now, a private who loses a rifle suffers far greater consequences than a general who loses a war.[73]

—LTC Paul Yingling

Much has been written about the risk-averse nature of our senior officer corps, including the excellent observations of Paul Yingling and Ralph Peters. The growth of a risk-averse senior officer corps has emasculated our warrior class more thoroughly than Stalin's purges of the Red Army prior to WWII. We have bred a timid, introverted cadre of officers who either lack the guts to stand up to our political leadership or who are all too willing to sell out their troops to advance their careers. Much of the blame can be attributed to the increasing inclusion of lawyers into the command decision cycle.

In the civilian community, once a lawyer gets his nose under the tent flap of an organization, his corpulent body will surely follow. Hence, there are more attorneys in Washington, D.C., than all of Japan. Sadly the military is following the lead of Washington rather than Japan. This is not to say that lawyers have no place in the military; perhaps no place more so than the enforcement of discipline. But they have become the catalyst of a plague that is eroding our nation's ability to conduct war. As former Secretary of Defense Donald Rumsfeld once said, "Reduce the number of lawyers. They are like beavers—they get in the middle of the stream and dam it up." Rumsfeld also questioned why the ratio of lawyers does not remain constant in a drawdown of forces. In some circles, Rumsfeld had a reputation of being a stubborn, wrong-headed toxic leader, but he was spot-on here.

A client's need for a lawyer is largely based on fear. Sometimes that fear is warranted, as when an accused soldier is facing jail time for an alleged criminal act. In such an instance it is prudent for that soldier to have an attorney. A fair justice system is an effective one.

In the risk-averse and labyrinthine organization that the military has become—especially during and after the personnel drawdown of the early nineties—a commander needs an attorney to successfully navigate the hazards in his quest for promotion. In the 1990s, when President Clinton was escalating the military drawdown initiated by the prior administration, the military fell back on tried-and-true methods of diminishing the size of the force. One of these methods was the threat of a reduction in force (RIF). The reduction in force had the effect of creating merciless critical evaluations that leave the recipient with no other option than to leave the service before being forced out. Despite various studies showing that force levels were dangerously low, the military continued to cut its forces. During this time period, a dangerous culture developed: the snapshot theory of leadership. This theory in reality is akin to the adage of "first impressions are lasting impressions." The military corollary to this is that you may have done one hundred exemplary things during your tenure in command, but if you did *one* thing that could be frowned upon or draw the ire of any of whom David Hackworth called the "Perfumed Princes," you were DRT (dead right there). One aggressive action-gone-bad would be officer evaluation report (OER) fodder and cause for ejection from the military. A second-order effect of this madness was that leaders soon learned to do nothing but hunker down and recite such aphorisms as "force protection" and "safety certifications" to cover their lack of warfighting aggressiveness. A Special Forces friend was in charge of an A-Team in the Balkans during this time. He wrote of how absolutely incensed he became at the rules his superiors foisted upon him: "If your team is hit at the base, run underground and let the host-nation forces protect you. *Do not* defend yourselves except in the direst of circumstances!" This, to a Green Beret warrior.

These observations of the pervasiveness of toxic leaders were validated by a Command and General Staff College (CGSC) study in the late nineties. The study observed falling morale, a virtually nonexistent esprit-de-corps, and a sense of hopelessness wrought by constant deployment as the world's "Peace Corps with Guns" (as the military affectionately called itself during the constant meddling and perceived do-gooding of the Clinton years) and the continuous bleeding of some of our most effective warfighting capabilities. The body of students at this prestigious midlevel education facility for officers documented that they were unsatisfied with their leaders. They felt their leaders would "toss them under the bus" if it led to career advancement for the senior officers.

These very same senior officers came to rely heavily upon the skills of their lawyers both to avoid career-ending personal pitfalls and to inflict career-ending administrative actions on their peers and subordinates. How did this happen? It was not a deliberate conspiracy by military attorneys to infect the system. In fact, most JAG officers are extremely patriotic and well-intentioned. Rather, it is the method by which some of these attorneys rationalize and reason that should be recognized as anathema to an effective, combat-ready organization. Clarity of purpose, unity of effort, and proper communication are essential to an effectively run military operation. Lawyers like to create gray areas and mistake complexity and uncertainty for intelligence. Instead of saying yes when they mean yes, or no when they mean no, lawyers will say something to the effect of the following when advising a battalion commander: "Well, sir, it's not that Second Lieutenant Smedlap did anything wrong per se, it's just that he has created an appearance of impropriety." For the appearance of impropriety, the lieutenant's career is tubed. The battalion commander, recognizing the danger of having his own career tubed if he does anything, no matter how trivial, which may create "an appearance of impropriety," starts consulting his legal advisor for everything. The JAG legal advisor can then report to his immediate superior, usually a division or corps staff judge advocate, that he is intimately involved in the battalion plans and operations. Everybody wins on his report card (save the poor lieutenant), but the battalion's go-to-war status is drastically impaired.

Take young Specialist-promotable Spree for example. (Name changed to protect the innocent.) Specialist Spree was assigned to 1-4 Infantry, the Opposition Forces (OPFOR) Battalion at the Combined Maneuver Training Center (CMTC) in Hohenfels, Germany. At the time, CMTC was one of the army's three computer-scored, life-sized training centers worldwide. The other two were the Joint Readiness Training Center (JRTC) at Fort Polk, Louisiana, and the National Training Center (NTC) at Fort Irwin, California. The development of these training centers was a positive result of the army's rededication to mission after the post-Vietnam drawdown. There is a full-time Opposition Force (OPFOR) cadre that plays the role of enemy forces for units rotating through the centers on training cycles. The OPFOR is usually tough and prideful by nature.

The commander of 1-4 had the reputation for routinely slam-dunking young soldiers at Article 15 proceedings (nonjudicial punishment proceedings) for the mildest infractions. Article 15s are one step below courts-martial in severity and basically come in two flavors: field grade and company grade. Field grade Article 15s, those imposed by commanders in the grade of major or higher, carry more serious punishment. Additionally, this commander did nothing to hide his disdain for lawyers.

Well, Spree was a young infantry soldier. His immediate chain of command was prepping him for promotion and ranger school. U.S. Army Ranger School is an approximately eleven-week intensive and exhausting program designed to produce some of the world's finest light infantry. Upon graduation, students are awarded the coveted Ranger Tab. The selection and assessment process, as well as successful graduation numbers, are discriminating. But the award of a Ranger Tab does not preclude the possibility of its bearer being a toxic leader.

Spree was about 6'2" tall, and built like the Terminator. He is exactly the type of soldier we want killing the enemy and breaking stuff when a war starts. Unfortunately, over the previous weekend, Spree and some buddies ended up drinking to excess in downtown Regensburg, the closest place to CMTC resembling a city. After getting totally trashed, the young soldiers began horsing around with each other. Spree picked up his buddy and threw him through a plate glass window at an Irish pub. Fortunately, no one was seriously injured. His buddy thought it was funny. Spree knew the bar owner and promised restitution.

Two days later, Spree made total restitution, and that should have been the end of the story. Not in 1-4 Infantry. Apparently an M.P. report was made, so the case ended up on the M.P. blotter, a daily report for commanders concerning the previous day's incidents. The battalion commander demanded an immediate field grade Article 15 be prepared for his signature. Spree stood the risk of losing all his rank, two-thirds of his basic pay for two months, as well as extra duty. This was known as maxing a soldier out.

Specialist Spree said, "I know the Old Man will max me out, so I want a court-martial." A soldier has the right to turn down an Article 15 and demand a trial by court-martial. A defense counsel, if a case was totally without merit or the government was lacking proof, would often advise a soldier to turn down an Article 15. Unfortunately for Spree, the facts of his case would probably get him convicted of a drunk and disorderly or an assault charge. It simply was not worth him getting a federal conviction, even if a court-martial panel would give him minimal punishment. Furthermore, even this battalion commander, given the caliber of soldier that Spree was and in light of the immediate restitution, should not have maxed him out. Spree, on advice of counsel, accepted the Article 15. He got maxed out.

The commander did more to hurt the combat readiness of the army than had he bent a main gun tube on an Abrams tank. You don't grow Specialist Sprees overnight, and they are worth their weight in gold in combat.

This zero-defect mentality is what really hosed Specialist Spree. In the old days, even for an officer, this would have been handled by a wink and a nod. Take Steve Lamb, a former army defense counsel who is now practicing in Los Angeles. Steve was probably one of the finest judge advocates, if not officers, in the army. He left the corps in 1994 and is flourishing in private practice. He was a former Special Forces detachment commander, Ranger and Special Forces-qualified officer, and a great lawyer. He represented, among others, First Sergeant Roberto Enrique Bryan, the 82nd Airborne paratrooper charged with murder for an alleged war crimes violation in Panama in December 1989 during Operation Urgent Fury. Steve helped get Bryan justly and properly acquitted.

When Steve was a young lieutenant in Korea, he threw a fellow officer through a plate glass window at the officer's club. He paid for the window and got an ass-chewing from his battalion commander and that was the end of it. Steve went on to Special Forces, becoming a detachment commander with 10th Special Forces Group in Beirut, Lebanon, in 1983, a funded legal education officer, and a great trial attorney. If Steve had committed his "crime" in the nineties rather than the late seventies, he would have been fragged by the system.

Another Article 15 case bears examination. This one was out of Vicenza, Italy. Vicenza was home to the 3-325 Airborne Infantry Regiment, the rapid response force of the U.S. Army's Southern European Task Force (SETAF). In this case, a young paratrooper was killed during a training jump. Apparently he drowned in a canal he landed in after jumping from a CH-47 Chinook helicopter. An exhaustive safety review determined that a convergence of many factors caused the accident, not the least of which was unseasonably heavy rains. The paratrooper was also blown away from the drop zone by fluky winds at higher altitudes. The young trooper tragically happened to be the only non-swimmer in the group.

True to the zero-defect mentality of the army, and in response to a congressional inquiry, somebody had to pay. On the day in question, a young stud of an infantry officer was the Assistant Drop Zone Safety Officer (ADZSO) for the jump. According to the procedural handbook for that particular drop zone, the ADZSO was supposed to perform a one-kilometer survey of the surrounding countryside to investigate for water hazards. This was not done, so he's guilty. Never mind that a similar one-kilometer reconnaissance had not been done in the previous twenty years of jumping at that drop zone. Never mind that the battalion commander had forced the jump because everyone was in need of a quarterly jump for pay purposes.

This officer ended up accepting the Article 15 imposed by the SETAF commander, and was hosed. If the commanding general had any sand, he would have dismissed the Article 15 and written a letter to the deceased paratrooper's family telling them their son died training to defend his country's national interests. It would have been the truth and the right thing to do. Instead the command could now point to whom they crucified in response to the congressional inquiry. They took a stud leader—a warrior, a solid "top block" performer, the "best lieutenant in my battalion" according to the commander of 3-325 AIR—and flushed him down the toilet for political reasons. Again, it is for reasons like this that the army runs the risk of becoming a paper tiger. It will be filled with leaders who are either too afraid to make decisions, too crafty politically to avoid controversy, or too gutless to fight or win.

This last reality is exemplified by the plight of Army Colonel Michael D. Steele. As a captain, he was a company commander in the 3rd Battalion, 75th Ranger Regiment during the 1993 Somalia mission depicted in the movie *Black Hawk Down*. As a brigade commander in Iraq with the 187th Infantry Regiment (Rakkasans) of the 101st Airborne Division, which returned from a tour of duty in the Salah ad Din province in Iraq in the autumn of 2006, he was investigated in relation to the alleged murders of three unarmed Iraqis during Operation Iron Triangle. The four soldiers charged in the case testified that Steele had instructed them to "kill all military-age males." Despite videotaped evidence that Steele never gave such instructions, he was formally reprimanded by then-Lieutenant General Peter W. Chiarelli, former commander of the Multi-National Force—Iraq (later Vice Chief of Staff of the Army). Apparently, as spelled out below, Steele was "too aggressive" in his methods.

When he landed in Iraq, in 2005, Steele was the only brigade commander there to have experienced sustained urban warfare before 9/11. He arrived with a clear sense of purpose: to subdue violence with violence, to hunt down and kill insurgents in a region of roughly ten thousand square miles within Salah ad Din province, which includes the cities of Samarra, Tikrit, and Bayji. Steele had memorized the faces of dozens of high-value targets in the region—al Qaeda operatives and other militants—and he inspected the bodies of people his soldiers killed, looking for tattoos and other identifying marks. He personified the motto that his brigade, numbering nearly four thousand men, had adopted during the war: "We give the enemy the maximum opportunity to give his life for his country."

Steele has since entered Army folklore as a cautionary figure—a man who travelled to a murderous place believing, as Conrad's Mr. Kurtz did, that with the "simple exercise of our will we can exert a power for good practically unbounded," but ultimately concluding it necessary to "exterminate all the brutes."

Even as top leaders in the Army reprimanded Steele, his immediate superiors praised him for running the best brigade in his division, and the military's Central Command issued his unit an award for combating terrorism.[74]

God forbid we instill aggressiveness and self-preservation in our commanders and their warriors. And God forbid anyone in the military sings
the well-deserved praises of a soldier like Mike Steele. A few short years
later, one of Michael Steele's protégés was thrown under the bus in
Afghanistan. His crime was not cowardice before the enemy or failure to
fight. Rather, as reported in the January 23, 2010, edition of the *Fayetteville Observer*:

> A Fort Bragg battalion commander and his top enlisted adviser
> were removed from their jobs in Afghanistan and sent home for
> using "poor judgment," an 82nd Airborne Division spokesman
> said Friday.
>
> Lt. Col. Frank Jenio and Command Sgt. Maj. Bert Puckett
> were leaders of the 2nd Battalion, 508th Parachute Infantry Regi-
> ment, part of the 82nd's 4th Brigade Combat Team, which
> deployed in August to Afghanistan.
>
> An investigation found their "actions were of poor judgment
> which fostered a command climate that was not consistent with
> our Army values," the spokesman, Lt. Col. Clarence Counts,
> wrote in an e-mail from Afghanistan in a response to questions.
> "We are a values-based and professional organization committed
> to Army values, and this change reflects a continuous commit-
> ment to adhere to the highest standards of excellence while main-
> taining good order and discipline."[75]

"Poor judgment," that insidious catchall phrase the army is infamous for
using when it can't really define what a person did wrong and that leaves
folks like Frank Jenio tarnished and banished, in this case had nothing to do
with his valor, leadership, and abilities in combat. Rather, let's examine what
a blogger close to the battalion says about the underlying situation:

> In combat, in Afghanistan, LTC Frank Jenio, West Point graduate,
> warrior and ass-kicker par excellence has been sacked along with
> the Command Sergeant Major and the operations staff. Why?
> Because of two slides on a motivational PowerPoint presentation:
> one misinterpreted as racist (two football players; one black, one
> white) and one as sexist (girl in bikini). Both slides put into the

presentation by a black guy and a Latino. The end of an 18-year stellar career for Jenio . . . the only battalion commander in the brigade who is humping with the troops in the field. The battalion is in an absolute uproar, everyone from the troops to the Family Readiness Group are raising hell, as everyone loved working for the guy.

Of more concern is the decision to place warriors like Mike Steele, Frank Jenio, and their bands of infantrymen into operational environments that are better suited to a police or constabulary force: again, using a blunt force instrument for precision surgery. Then, after seeing the trauma this affects on the body, these same senior leaders express outrage and remorse over the fact that people are killed. They then proceed to excoriate patriots like Colonel Mike Steele and Lieutenant Colonel Frank Jenio.

Reflect upon the words of a letter purported to have been written by the Duke of Wellington in response to the meddlers of his day:

Gentlemen:

Whilst marching from Portugal to a position which commands the approach to Madrid and the French forces, my officers have been diligently complying with your requests, which have been sent by H.M. ship from London to Lisbon and thence by dispatch rider to our headquarters.

We have enumerated our saddles, bridles, tents and tent poles, and all manner of sundry items for which His Majesty's Government holds me accountable. I have dispatched reports on the character, wit, and spleen of every officer. Each item and every farthing have been accounted for, with two regrettable exceptions for which I beg your indulgence.

Unfortunately, the sum of one shilling and ninepence remains unaccounted for in one infantry battalion's petty cash and there has been hideous confusion as to the number of jars of raspberry jam issued to one cavalry regiment during a sandstorm in western Spain. This reprehensible carelessness may be related to the pressure of circumstances, since we are at war with France, a fact which may come as a bit of a surprise to you gentlemen at Whitehall.

This brings me to my present purpose, which is to request elucidation of my instruction from His Majesty's Government, so that I may better understand why I am dragging an army over these barren plains. I construe that perforce it must be one of two alternative duties, as given below. I shall pursue either one with my best ability, but I cannot do both.

1. To train an army of uniformed British clerks in Spain for the benefit of accountants and copy-boys in London, or, perchance
2. To see to it that the forces of Napoleon are driven out of Spain.

Your most obedient servant,

Wellington

CHAPTER EIGHT

The Safety Nazis

Dateline Balad, Iraq. Early 2006.

During a nighttime combat helicopter assault to capture or kill an al Qaeda leader, unpredictable bad weather forced the special ops helicopter to set down at Balad Air Base in Iraq. These troops had "been out in the wilds for quite a while," and they took the opportunity to go get some sundries from Balad's Base Exchange (BX). One of the safety rules at the time was that if you are on the base, you must wear a reflective belt at all times. As these hardened warriors—the best of the best—were en route to do some killing, they felt it inappropriate to attire themselves in Day-Glo yellow during night operations. Nonetheless, the warriors—numb to the military bureaucracy—figured that while at the BX they would purchase and then wear the safety belts according to the base commander's dictates. No complaining: This is what professional soldiers do.

While attempting to enter the facility they were confronted and stopped by a young soldier guarding the BX. Despite the fact that the BX was inside the wire, or on an already secure base, the young guard was burdened down with more accoutrements and body armor than the SOF operators had been carrying for their combat mission that night.

The following Catch-22 colloquy ensued: "I am Master Sergeant Smith," explained the warrior, displaying his military identification card, thinking that the young MP might not recognize him due to the fact that he was sporting the heavy stubble and nonstandard uniform typical of many special operations forces at the time.

"I recognize you, but you can't come in, sergeant," said the guard.

"Why not?"

"Because you aren't wearing a reflective safety belt, and the base commander has ordered that all personnel must wear a reflective safety belt 24-7 while on base," answered the guard.

"I know," replied the warrior, "that's why I am here, to buy a safety belt."

"But you can't come in without a safety belt . . . that's the colonel's orders . . . sorry, sarge." The operator left without a belt or sundries.

If this were a one-time example of an overzealous and overly cautious senior leader in our military, there would be no cause for alarm. Unfortunately it is becoming the norm.

One can barely maneuver around an American-controlled base in Iraq or Afghanistan without tripping over clearing barrels emplaced because of the paralyzing and obsessive concern the military has over accidental or negligent discharges of small arms. This obsession is unwarranted because the danger posed by accidental discharges pales in comparison to the threat of not having a weapon at the ready when a true danger arises, such as during Nidal Hasan's attack; or when a disgruntled Afghan pilot killed eight unarmed trainers in April 2011; or when two unarmed air force airmen were killed in Germany by a local *muj* in April 2011.

Moreover, instances of accidental discharges can be greatly attenuated by simple, yet comprehensive and realistic training. On the streets of America, 200,000 police officers walk around with loaded and holstered weapons, generally without a problem. In war zones, however, soldiers coming back onto base—regardless of their age, rank, or level of experience (to include the aforementioned Special Forces professional)—must remove their safely holstered weapons from the holster, manipulate them in a crowded area, and clear (unload) them with barrels pointed into the sand-filled clearing barrels. And when a weapon does, on occasion, fire into a clearing barrel—isn't that why they have clearing barrels?—the command generally crucifies the guilty party with a career-ending Article 15 or letter of reprimand.

Within the Green Zone in Iraq, despite the threat of insurgent attack, soldiers are not allowed to have a loaded weapon. In fact, they are forced to carry their weapons with no magazine in their weapon's magazine wells. Despite the lunacy prescribed by the policy of carrying an unloaded weapon in a war zone, they still must go through the ridiculous pantomime of clearing an unloaded weapon into clearing barrels before entering every building.

This safety panic has gotten so bad that a command sergeant major from a Special Forces unit recently reported that he knows of some senior leaders who fake charging their weapons when they go outside the wire so that they avoid the potential for an accidental discharge upon their return to base. Many military members have reportedly been forced to place strips of colored tape over their magazine wells to visually show that their weapons are unloaded.

Again, this group that calls itself the armed forces has gradually and consistently developed a fear and vilification of weapons. On any given day, one can observe sergeants major or command chiefs (the highest enlisted ranks in the military) standing on street corners on bases in Iraq checking to see if the drivers of passing military vehicles are wearing seatbelts on streets already hamstrung by 15 mph speed limits. On the aforementioned Balad Air Base, military police used radar against military personnel driving above the posted speed limits. At the same time, Balad was rocketed and mortared every single morning and night for forty-five days straight, while military police handed out speeding tickets for driving too fast! Besides being laughable, this is hardly an efficient use of experienced military leaders, who are supposed to be advising general and field grade officers on the conduct of the mission and effectiveness of their fighting force.

Here, at training bases in the United States, realistic firearms training is consistently stymied due to illegitimate concerns. Soldiers, sailors, airmen, and marines—except those assigned to elite units—rarely, if ever, are allowed to practice shoot-on-the-move techniques, combat reloads, or other tactical engagement scenarios due to overzealous safety concerns. Anyone who has ever shot on a military range has heard the constant range control mantra, "Keep your weapons pointed up and downrange, don't load until directed by the tower," and so on, forgetting all the time that there is no "up and downrange" in Iraq. More important, the enemy is never a readily identifiable static target just waiting to be shot on command.

Attempts to introduce innovative and realistic training methodologies like the use of Simunitions (nonlethal training ammunition—essentially glorified paint balls—fired from the soldiers' weapons that can deliver effective threat identification and tactical training) or shoot on the move live-fire techniques are most often met with stiff resistance or outright naysaying by those in command or in charge of range control. This naysaying is rooted in either a "not invented here" mentality or woeful ignorance of modern training methodologies. Senior leaders, when confronted with novel training approaches, too often rely on what they experienced twenty years earlier as junior platoon leaders. Effective training is only allowed to proceed when senior leaders who are not prone to risk-averse thinking become aware of the problem and correct it.

Some officers and noncommissioned officers have made careers as safety officers. Monthly magazines are published in all four services with myriad new checklists and safety methodologies. It has gotten so bad that one can't run innovative and more realistic weapons training without running afoul of the latest nonsense. This over-the-top type of safety first mentality is yet more evidence of America's generation of risk-averse officers. This is dangerous because it is contrary to developing a warrior mentality and it degrades realistic training.

This cover-your-butt style of leadership impairs the military systemically because everyone is too busy looking over their shoulders instead of focusing on what should be the military's real mission: to seek and kill those who would do America harm. Similarly the mission becomes so watered down by legalisms that it is nearly unrecognizable. "War" became "peace enforcement," and "enemy" became "hostile force." The results over the past two decades (certainly during the Clinton era) have been battalion commanders coming back from a tour in Kosovo, Bosnia, and now, even Iraq or Afghanistan, describing their mission as a success because "no one had to fire a shot!" or "we always used minimum force!" Very dangerous definitions of mission success: Sometimes our mission requires a vigorous self-defense, and sometimes our mission means killing lots of people.

Also the sad truth is that many of our nation's finest warriors have been booted out of the military because of the zero-defect mentality. As an example, a young noncommissioned officer, ranger-qualified, master parachutist, and a true leader had his career terminated because of one off-duty indiscretion. The brain dead who march lockstep to the zero-defect tune say, "True leaders don't misbehave" or "Poor judgment can't be tolerated." Besides being a circular argument, this self-fulfilling mantra has resulted in a large corps of mediocre warriors who never take chances. Moreover, at the senior level, these leaders seem to be self-selecting. In other words, a "break glass in time of war" leader who may not be a warrior-diplomat or who may not "maneuver seamlessly in the interagency environment" will be passed over for promotion.

CHAPTER NINE

The Expansive Role of Counsel

There was a time not so long ago, when camaraderie, esprit de corps, and warrior mentalities dominated. Things began to change drastically in the 1980s, and by the time the 1990s and its reduction in force (RIF) rolled around, the politically correct, zero-defect mentality was really gearing up. Unfortunately, it would only get worse.

The role of lawyers at the strategic, operational, and even tactical levels has introduced a degree of oversight that is at once unnecessary and corrosive. This oversight has inundated all aspects of the Department of Defense: personnel, acquisition, and operational.

On one occasion, the Joint IED Defeat Organization (JIEDDO)—a hybrid organization with an annual budget of around $4 billion that was chartered in 2006 to combat the strategic threat posed by Improvised Explosive Devices (IEDs) and reports directly to the Deputy Secretary of Defense—built a village in the deserts of Fort Irwin that mirrored the architectural characteristics of an Iraqi village. This Iraqi village project was used to test the efficacy of multiple counter-IED electronic platforms that JIEDDO was constantly testing. JIEDDO used Research, Development, Test and Evaluation (RDT&E) funds to pay for the village test site. All of this, of course, would make perfect sense to most Americans. JIEDDO is researching, developing, and testing new equipment to save soldiers' lives: use RDT&E money, right?

At the time, the army was the executive agency for JIEDDO, responsible for many of its mundane administrative support needs. Some lawyers at Headquarters Department of the Army (HQDA) said that the construction of such a village should have used military construction (MILCON) funding—an extremely cumbersome, two-year funding process—and that JIEDDO's use of RDT&E funding constituted an Anti-Deficiency Act violation. In other words, someone might be criminally liable for authorizing the use of these funds. So started a yearlong investigation! This led author Bolgiano, when Deputy General Counsel for JIEDDO, to write in response to one of the HQDA missives: "If America fought World War II with the same degree of timidity and legal oversight, we would all be speaking German now."

Just as America has become paralyzed with lawsuits, so has our military. The air force—in desperate need of replacing its fleet of KC-135 tankers, which now average over fifty years old—has been mired in a procurement nightmare mostly caused by lawyer-led bid protests and legal oversight restrictions. Can you imagine if the procurement of B-17s and B-29s in World War II were subject to such byzantine and debilitating rules?

While there may be plausible arguments to be made in favor of such restrictive legal oversight at the procurement end of the machine, such degree of scrutiny has filtered down to the actual tip of the spear. At one point, the legal staff at Multi-National Corps Iraq (MNC-I) called a special operations force unit to query, "Under what theory are you seizing the computers of the suspects you are capturing?" Thinking this was a joke, the SOF lawyer laughed aloud and said, "Good one." The MNC-I headquarters lawyer again said, "We need to know the legal theory under which you are seizing the computers and data-processing equipment of the terrorists!" The SOF lawyer politely replied that when MNC-I could legitimately articulate a rationale that would embody terrorists to enjoy the freedom to retain the tools of their terror, he would answer his question. What's shocking is that this subject had been prevalent at such a high level for some time. When did we turn the art of war into the prosecution of criminals with all its attendant rules of criminal procedure? Not surprisingly, warrant-based targeting, in which American commanders must seek the judicial approval of Iraqi courts before killing or capturing al Qaeda, is now in effect.

The conduct of war by lawyers, and its resultant weakening of the morale and warrior-like ethos of our force, is also clearly exemplified by an HQDA investigation of a Special Operations Command Central (SOC-CENT) commander that occurred after that command's highly successful exploits in the initial invasion of Iraq in 2003. By way of background, U.S. forces have historically returned to their home bases with war trophies and symbols of their success over vanquished foes. Ardennes Street, the home of the famed 82nd Airborne Division in Fort Bragg, North Carolina, has excellent examples of such artifacts. Peering into the brigade headquarters of the famed 504th Parachute Infantry Regiment, you can see Nazi memorabilia and trophies from World War II or anti-aircraft guns and other weaponry taken from Manuel Noriega's Panamanian Defense Forces from Operation Just Cause in December 1989.

World War II veterans from the Pacific brought back shiploads of Japanese bayonets, rifles, flags, swords, and uniforms. No one would dare question the capture, or propose the return, of such memorabilia by American fighting forces. It is a well-earned right and privilege of those risking their lives to bring home some tangible remembrance of those vanquished. As exemplified by the following not-so-uncommon horror story, the meddlers and hand-wringers masquerading as leaders are working overtime to destroy this time-honored and important practice.

In April and May 2003, SOCCENT forces captured enemy equipment and property, including brand new weapons (AK-47s and Russian-designed machine guns), some cheap gold-plated ceremonial weapons, and diverse rugs and a portrait of Saddam captured from his former palaces in and around Baghdad International Airport. SOCCENT prominently declared all these items to its higher headquarters, and even received permission from Commander, Central Command, General Tommy Franks, to bring these items home for the express purpose of (1) replenishing the depleted or worn-out weapons at the John F. Kennedy Special Warfare Center at Fort Bragg (the command responsible for, among other things, training our nations' Special Forces or Green Berets) and (2) display at SOCCENT Headquarters at MacDill AFB in Tampa, Florida. None of the above would constitute a criminal offense. There has been over two hundred years of historical precedence in America of doing the same thing. Never let reason, the law, or historical precedence get in the way of political correctness and New Age globalism. And never underestimate the power of judge advocates to provide ill-advised and ahistoric advice that causes meddlers to go into high gear.

Two months after SOCCENT's redeployment from Iraq to MacDill AFB, unnamed sources (later identified as two disgruntled subordinates) filed an Inspector General complaint with HQDA alleging that Commander SOCCENT and members of his staff "stole items from the Iraqi people." Instead of summarily dismissing such a claim on its face, or resolving it with a few simple phone calls to the commander or his legal staff, HQDA referred the matter to the Army Criminal Investigation Division (CID) Command's Field Investigation Unit (FIU), a unit normally assigned to investigate suspected criminal matters within the military's black or special mission unit world. This was supposedly done because of Commander SOCCENT's prior life in the black world and the tangential involvement of a special mission unit in the retrieval of one of the "gold-plated" weapons from Saddam's palace (actually it was his son Udey Hussein's palace).

After months of investigation in which rights warnings were read to the commander and members of his staff, including his lawyer, it was pretty clear that no criminal offense occurred, but a judge advocate assigned to the FIU said that the commander committed the offense of larceny. Even a first year law school student knows that the elements of larceny require a person to specifically intend to permanently deprive another of their property. When SOCCENT seized the property in question it became, as a matter of law, the property of the United States of America. Commander SOCCENT had a duty to return it to the United States. To do otherwise would have been a dereliction of that duty.

But this lawyer substituted her own notions of geopolitical righteousness—that these guns and war trophies belonged to the Iraqi people—and her ill-founded legal opinion led to twelve months of further and unnecessary investigation into the SOCCENT personnel involved. It also unnecessarily attempted to tarnish the reputation of one of America's finest warriors.

An interesting historical footnote to the incident is that CID supposedly lost one of the gold-plated weapons it seized from the Fort Belvoir headquarters of the Special Mission Unit, an ornately engraved Smith & Wesson Model 27 presented to Kuwait by the Kingdom of Saudi Arabia in 1986 and seized by Saddam Hussein in his 1990 invasion of Kuwait.

You can only imagine that it is hanging as a war trophy on a wall of that CID unit or in the basement of one of its agents.

The folly of investigating one of America's few general officers who has experienced the close-up personal violence of combat, to say nothing of the complete fraud, waste, and abuse of funds and authority by those conducting the investigation, is symptomatic of the invasion and institutionalization of lawyer-think into the Department of Defense. The knee-jerk reaction by many lawyers to any claim—no matter how specious—is to investigate it. In doing so, any complaint—including those made by slackers, internal enemies, or fifth columnists—can unleash a storm of controversy, innuendo, and appearances of impropriety that paralyzes our warfighting ability. Yet time and again military lawyers advise their commanders, "If an allegation is raised, you must investigate."

At another level, the attitudes and perspectives of both the complainants and some of the investigators reveal a major shortcoming in our war strategy. The fact that these folks sincerely believed that the property seized by SOCCENT was the property of the Iraqi people demonstrates just how far we have strayed from inculcating a warrior state of mind in our force. We have bred and encouraged a generation of sheep rather than sheepdogs. Hopefully America will not suffer a domestic nuclear event or a loss to a strong conventional force like China before America realizes that warriors must be steely-eyed killers and not diplomats.

The military has also chosen to go down a dangerous path vis-à-vis its treatment of civilian contractors, especially in the field of logistics. Due to the drawdown of the 1990s and the A-76 movement that caused an explosive growth in the use of contractors, the Department of Defense has become nearly totally reliant upon contractor support of its logistics and sustainment infrastructure. The A-76 program is governed by Office of Management and Budget (OMB) Circular A-76, "Performance of Commercial Activities." The basic tenet of the A-76 program is that functions should be performed in the most efficient and cost-effective way regardless of whether that is with government employees or contractor personnel. It is highly doubtful that the program, as implemented, has ever conformed to this basic tenet. Unfortunately the armed forces' commitment to protecting and disciplining contractors has been derelict. This is especially true in the area of arming civilian contractors.

In a panic born of perceived instances of excessive force, such as with the Blackwater case, many commands are severely restricting the ability for U.S. contract personnel, many of them former military members, to defend themselves in hostile fire zones. Moreover, when there are instances when the use of force in self-defense is questioned, there has been a growing tendency to treat such cases as criminally focused civilian investigations. These investigations carry the potential of trial by Article 3 courts (U.S. district courts) as opposed to Article 1 courts (military courts-martial). This blending of judicial with martial will only weaken the martial qualities of our force. Contractors, now afraid of criminal and civil liability, will be hesitant to accompany the force and provide the requisite logistical support. Just as medical malpractice lawsuits here have raised the cost of medical treatment, such exposure will surely increase the costs for such contractor support, thereby increasing the already bloated costs of any expedition.

The knee-jerk reaction of many military leaders and lawyers is to severely restrict the ability of American contractors to carry firearms in hostile fire areas. This is a crying shame and a dereliction of duty. These same lawyers—who want to limit former special mission unit warriors from carrying arms for self-defense when they are acting as contractors—fail to see the irony and hypocrisy of themselves being armed under similar circumstances. Why would anyone try to prevent a fellow American from arming himself in Iraq or Afghanistan? The answer is threefold: they fundamentally do not understand the laws and tactics of self-defense; they are as risk-averse as their commanders; and they place the same value on the lives of Americans as they do on the *muj*.

CHAPTER TEN

Understanding the Law of Self-Defense

One ought never to turn one's back on a threatened danger and try to run away from it. If you do that, you will double the danger. But if you meet it promptly and without flinching, you will reduce the danger by half. Never run away from anything. Never![76]
—Winston S. Churchill

There is misunderstanding—even among otherwise learned judge advocates—concerning the robust legal authority in which individual soldiers, sailors, airmen, and marines may use force in self-defense. It is important, therefore, to first comprehend the depth and breadth of the law in this regard, as well as its relevance to military operations.

At a strategic level, the lawful authority, domestically and internationally, for United States forces to use force is rooted in the right of self-defense. By keeping all uses of military power—specifically war and warlike actions—founded in self-defense, America will retain the moral high ground, clearly signal its strategic intentions to potential adversaries, and avoid straying into the morass of commitments not rooted in self-defense. This applies to the individual's right of self-defense as well.

From seemingly benign humanitarian assistance missions to hard-fought counterinsurgency operations, most of the decisions our forces make are predicated on the right of self-defense. Applying such decisions in the "three block war"[77] environment—wherein warriors might face a determined foe in one block, a humanitarian assistance victim in the next block, and an armed gang with unknown intentions in the last—requires our strategic corporals to individually and near-intuitively understand their rights and authorities to use force in self-defense.

In order to fully appreciate the right of self-defense, it is worth examining its historical roots. Consistently, since at least 60 B.C., laws and customs have recognized individuals' inherent right to reasonably defend themselves from an attacker threatening to inflict death or serious bodily injury. Historically, the right of self-defense has been viewed not as a statutory or legal right, but as a divine natural right permanently bestowed on all persons by virtue of existence. Over 2,000 years ago Marcus Tullius Cicero wrote:

> There does exist therefore, gentlemen, a law which is a law not of the statute-book, but of nature; a law which we possess not by instruction, tradition, or reading, but which we have caught, imbibed, and sucked in at Nature's own breast; a law which comes to us not by education but by constitution, not by training but by intuition—the law, I mean, that should our life have fallen into any snare, into the violence and the weapons of robbers or foes, every method of winning a way to safety would be morally justifiable.[78]

William Blackstone, the father of English common law, wrote, "Self defense is justly called the primary law of nature, so it is not, neither can it be in fact, taken away by the laws of society."[79] "The right of having and using arms for self-preservation and defense" is one of the five auxiliary rights people possess to "protect and maintain 'the three great and primary rights, personal security, personal liberty, and private property."[80]

English philosopher John Locke observed, "self defense is a part of the law of nature, nor can it be denied the community, even against the king himself."[81] In his treatise on civil government, self-defense is fundamental to the very existence of mankind. Much like one is justified in killing a wild animal if it displays intent to attack, one is justified in taking the life of another person if that person displays intent to do harm to you. Locke reasoned:

One may destroy a man who makes war upon him, or has discovered an enmity to his being, for the same reason that he may kill a wolf or a lion; because such men are not under the ties of the common law of reason, have no other rule, but that of force and violence, and so may be treated as beasts of prey, those dangerous and noxious creatures, that will be sure to destroy him whenever he falls into their power.[82]

English common law long recognized an individual's right to self-defense as a natural and divine right.[83] The Founding Fathers used English common law as a platform to build the U.S. Constitution. The drafters were heavily influenced by the works of William Blackstone and drafted the core of the Constitution to protect life, liberty, and property. Self-defense was a part of the right to personal security, as one could not be secure in his safety without the right to defend against those wishing to deprive him of it.[84] Mirroring Blackstone's statements, Samuel Adams wrote: "Among the natural rights of the Colonists are these: First, a right to life; Secondly, to liberty; Thirdly, to property; together with the right to support and defend them in the best manner they can."[85] The Constitution reflects Blackstone's influence in the Bill of Rights, which explicitly protects our rights to life, liberty, and property, and freedom from government intrusion. This constitutional robustness of the inherent right of self-defense is the lynchpin of the social contract between the government and its citizenry.

Even under international legal constructs, it should be noted that customary and statutory international law recognizes the inherent right of self-defense. On such fundamental concerns as self-defense, America may enter into short- or long-term alliances but must never submit to the will of the collective international masses when discerning what constitutes a justifiable act of self-defense. This is because collective thought might reflect collective ignorance. This is evidenced by the restrictions imposed by the United Nations that have plagued General Bipin Rawat, an Indian officer who commands UN forces in Democratic Republic of Congo:

Under their rules of engagement, Gen Rawat's forces are always denied the advantage of surprise. They must shout verbal warnings and fire shots in the air before they can engage any rebels. Their operations are not allowed to risk a single civilian casualty.[86]

One glowing ember of hope in the darkness of such ill-conceived UN-authored rules of engagement (ROE) is that such rules apply to the targeting of forces rather than using force in individual or collective self-defense. Accordingly there remains strong constitutional, common law, and international law support for both collective and individual rights of self-defense. In all missions—from humanitarian relief operations to force-on-force conflict—America can justly and lawfully support uses of force in self-defense. This extends to the rules as they apply to the individual soldier, sailor, airman, or marine.

Despite mandatory guidance from the Chairman, Joint Chiefs of Staff, that "commanders, at all levels, shall ensure that individuals within their respective units understand and are trained on when and how to use force in self-defense,"[87] the dangerous, and sometimes tragic, reality is that this mandate is not being well-carried out by the services, often in the ill-founded belief that the counterinsurgency fight requires our forces to "take the first shot" from our enemies before returning fire. Also many soldiers, sailors, airmen, and marines are not properly trained on threat recognition and appropriate tactical responses to a hostile act or demonstration of hostile intent. This creates not only a heightened risk for friendly forces, but also a greater likelihood of uses of force that might undermine strategic success, especially in the counterinsurgency fight.

CHAPTER ELEVEN

Using Deadly Force in Military Operations

Commanders and warriors are always looking for simple, direct, and easily applied ROE that answer their fundamental use-of-force question: "When should I pull the trigger?" While general guidelines for upper command levels can be set forth in the ROE Annex of an Operations Order, and even more particular guidance handed out to subordinate echelons via ROE cards, the answer to such a question is almost always incident specific and must be based on the split-second judgment of the individual on the scene. In such situations ROE cards and Escalation of Force (EOF) cards remain nearly useless (and often needlessly dangerous) as they assume a linear linkage in a nonlinear world. Paralleling the problem that critics of effects-based operations have identified—that the "nearly limitless ways that an action might ricochet through an interactively complex or nonlinear system mean that for all practical purposes, the interactions within the system exceed the calculative capacities for any computer to follow, at least in any meaningful way"[88]—ROE or EOF cards ignore the fact that deadly force situations are complex and not conducive to if-then solutions. ROE cards make poor field expedient toilet paper and even less efficacious legal and tactical guidance. Yet they remain ubiquitous in the modern force. Commanders like them as talismans or proof that they briefed the ROE to their troops and judge advocates like them as evidence of their contribution to the fight. Neither party explores the option of training forces correctly and adequately (more evidence of the violation of Occam's razor).

There are also recurring misunderstandings by many service members and judge advocates concerning the level and degree of authority needed to engage lawful targets. This misunderstanding and confusion leads to the mistaken belief that the actual status of an individual shot in self-defense must first be ascertained. Too often warriors are briefed that they must have PID (positive identification) before engaging. Such ill-founded beliefs are perpetuated by the repeated use of criminally-focused investigations into what are, in essence, line-of-duty shooting decisions.

Killing another without lawful authority constitutes murder, manslaughter, or negligent homicide. This applies in the military, too. There are several manners by which a military member can lawfully employ deadly force, such as defense of certain classified facilities or property, but the most relevant and prevalent two are discussed here. The first is subject to a target being declared hostile by competent authority and the second is in response to a demonstrated hostile intent or hostile act (intended to inflict death or serious bodily injury to self or friendly forces).

Declarations of a hostile force come from the highest levels of government: generally the president and secretary of defense. Such declarations specifically designate an enemy force or group. Now unclassified, members of the Iraqi military, certain paramilitary groups, and designated alphabet soup of terrorist organizations were designated as hostile forces during the initial phase of Operation Iraqi Freedom in 2003.

Against a declared hostile, once PID is established, then there is no legal obligation to detain, capture, or otherwise take less intrusive means in engaging that target. And they are—indeed—a target. A soldier could walk into a barracks room filled with sleeping enemy combatants who have been declared hostile and shoot them. There is no legal obligation to wake them, capture them, or make it a fair fight. Similarly if a tactical operations center can lawfully drop a 2,000-pound laser-guided bomb on that barracks room, then a lone soldier should be able to kill them with his M-4. One need look no further than the furor over the killing of bin Laden to illustrate this. For some reason, however, when some judge advocates and commanders review these close-in killing situations, they become squeamish and mistakenly analyze them under a self-defense methodology as set forth below.

In matters of individual or unit self-defense, as spelled out in the unclassified portions of the Standing Rules of Engagement (SROE) and

Standing Rules for the Use of Force (SRUF) for U.S. Forces,[89] service members possess an inherent right of self-defense predicated solely on a reasonable response to a demonstrated hostile intent or hostile act (intended to inflict death or serious bodily injury to self or friendly forces). In self-defense situations, PID is irrelevant, as it matters little if the threat is a hard-core member of al Qaeda or a crazed pizza delivery man, and proportionality is rarely an issue. Soldiers need to understand that they can use reasonable force to quell such a threat until that threat is over. As the marines say, "Shoot them into the ground."

Misunderstanding these rules breeds unnecessary confusion and hesitation among the force. This confusion results not only in unnecessary risks to our forces but also in our young warriors' persistent exposure to criminal liability for the perceived crime of killing the enemy. We mistakenly equate American lives with those of the enemy. Again we should take to heart Winston Churchill's quote, "I refuse to remain neutral between the fire and the fire brigade."

For years now, nearly every line-of-duty shooting incident in Iraq has been subject to an often criminally focused investigation whereby sworn statements are taken and service members are questioned without the benefit of legal counsel, psychologists, or chaplains. While it is necessary for proper discipline to ensure that service members follow the rules and use force appropriately—i.e., no wanton killing of civilian noncombatants as occurred at My Lai—the perception and reality is that continually subjecting our forces to the wrong legal standard and improperly focused investigations inevitably results in hesitation and mistrust. The following October 2007 communiqué from a young army noncommissioned officer in Iraq highlights this:

> There is nothing to come of this except making my Soldiers scared to pull the trigger and that's all that this is doing. They see me getting questioned every day over something as dumb as firing back when fired upon. God only knows what they would be trying to do if we accidentally killed one [of] the "wrong" people.[90]

Another noncommissioned officer—a sniper—was recently court-martialed over the killing of three Iraqis suspected, among other things, of emplacing IEDs. While he and his team possessed the legal authority to kill the targeted individuals, without understanding their inherent authority, they mistakenly believed they had to plant evidence on bodies after what were in reality legitimate kills. This perception results directly from failing to properly educate our forces on the legal authority extant for making judgment-based shooting decisions and conducting criminally focused investigations on soldiers' decisions to use force in combat. The sniper was acquitted of the murder charges but convicted of obstruction of justice for planting evidence.[91]

An infantry battalion commander who returned from Iraq in 2008 voiced his frustration with the tactical/legal policy in the following account:

My battalion along with other elements of my BCT [Brigade Combat Team] spent six months training up for our OIF [Operation Iraqi Freedom] rotation. We completed the mandatory training events to include a JRTC [Joint Readiness Training Center] rotation preparing us well for "full spectrum" kinetic and non-kinetic operations at the tactical and operational levels. When we would have an escalation of force that involved any shots fired, it was a CCIR [Commanders Critical Incident Report] to my higher headquarters. Initially the BCT SJA [Staff Judge Advocate] would review each incident and recommend that the BCT Commander issue letters of concern to Soldiers for any and all EOF's [escalations of force]. This practice confused and frustrated my Soldiers. These young men were working in difficult, challenging, and potentially deadly situations. In my opinion it did not require a legal review for every EOF that had warning shots fired. In every case that I reviewed regarding an EOF they were doing the right thing with all the right intentions, and doing what they needed to do to protect themselves and others in the unit. I was eventually able to get through to the BCT Commander that the SJA was applying a CYA [cover your ass], one-size-fits-all mentality from the comfort of his air-conditioned office. These letters of concern from the BCT Commander made my Soldiers and my unit more vulnerable to frustration and hesitation in a dangerous game in which you can't just stick in a green key and do it over.[92]

Sniper teams in Iraq or Afghanistan performing counter-IED missions may engage persons conducting overt hostile acts (such as actively emplacing an IED in a roadway surface) or persons demonstrating hostile intent (a lookout using a cell phone while communicating the approach of coalition forces), both clear examples of using force in self-defense. That same team may also be employed to engage a designated hostile force or enemy combatant and may engage without regard as to whether that hostile force presents an imminent threat.

This concept extends to fleeing subjects previously identified as hostile by adjacent friendly forces or who self-identify as being a hostile as when the ROE in force says words to the effect of "all members of al Qaeda in Iraq and 'those actively assisting them' can be engaged." This is exactly what happened to a unit when, due to the tactical situation, they could not immediately engage a subject they witnessed emplacing an IED. They were unable to immediately engage this subject when the bad guy triggered the IED on the unit. However, days later, one of the patrol members saw the same subject in the marketplace. The subject had very distinctive and recognizable facial features. Rapid discussion on the spot led the patrol to let the *muj* get away as he "wasn't currently a threat." During a discussion with the frustrated legal NCOs of that unit, one of the authors explained that both under the rules of self-defense and the ROE—the fact that terrorist had identified himself as a hostile—the terrorist could be killed. The NCO replied, "Yeah, I hear ya, but the command ain't gonna like this." Just what was there not to like? See a terrorist, shoot him dead. Simple. But not in the minds of the New Age poseurs we have in command of some units who would otherwise say, "But he doesn't have a weapon"; or "there was no imminence to the threat." Tough. This is war, not a playground game of tag. Yet, too often, this game-of-tag mentality is what passes as legal advice and command judgment in our war on terror.

Some commanders have even been reluctant to authorize the shooting of insurgents clearly emplacing IEDs in roadways late at night. They have prevented the targeting of insurgents conducting probes of friendly positions (like early probes by Mahdi militia of marine positions in Fallujah) and have also failed to authorize the kinetic engagement of clearly identified hostile vehicles speeding away from a mortar "point of origin" as they "were not a threat at the time of acquisition."[93]

This last point is important to clarify as some less tactically aware judge advocates and commanders have said that "fleeing hostile actors can't be engaged." To so state ignores at least three legal and tactical realities: the vehicle and occupants clearly identified themselves as hostile by firing mortars at U.S. forces; the concept of pursuit; and the hard reality that such a fleeing subject continues to be a threat. To put it even more bluntly: Nothing in the law allows a hostile actor to fire a weapon at coalition forces and then drop the weapon and flee without fear of being targeted and killed. Even in civilian law enforcement settings, such fleeing hostile actors are well recognized as a continuing threat that may be engaged.[94]

Some perhaps well-intentioned but ill-informed judge advocates have recently said that "one of the most effective ways to drive home the importance of EOF to soldiers [such as exercising fire discipline] at traffic control points and on convoys is by giving awards to soldiers who DO NOT SHOOT when the ROE may have allowed them to, thereby saving innocent lives."[95] The intent of this guidance—to save innocent civilian lives—might be admirable in a prayer service, but the end result of incorrectly trying to apply the strategic concept of minimum force to a tactical situation is to unnecessarily expose military forces to imminent threat of death or serious bodily injury. Missions are often ambiguous and dangerous enough; neither good tactics nor the law require a soldier surrender the right and responsibility to exercise either individual or collective self-defense. You have to question the judgment of anyone who would want to walk a patrol with someone who has been given medals for *not* firing at the enemy.

Many times, judge advocates assigned to special operations force commands find creative and cutting-edge solutions to perceived legal impediments in order to give the warriors assigned to such commands a better opportunity for mission success. Unfortunately, many times these judge advocates are accused by the JAG superiors of going native. This is supposed to be a pejorative—and in the hidebound depths of the Pentagon one might suppose it is—but judge advocates assigned to such units that don't go native most likely don't understand the mission. Moreover they most likely will not achieve the trust and confidence of their fellow warriors within that unit.

As stated by Major General Gary L. Harrell, USA (Ret.), former Deputy Commanding General, U.S. Army Special Operations Command, "The only tactical solution when confronted with an imminent threat of death or serious bodily injury is to immediately respond with overwhelming force and continue to apply that force until the threat is over."[96] Too often commanders and judge advocates with little or no true close quarters combat experience attempt to substitute their own notions of reasonableness for the warrior on the scene. The Supreme Court of the United States has consistently recognized this as folly for our domestic police forces:

> Such reasonableness must be judged from the perspective of a reasonable officer on the scene, rather than with the 20/20 vision of hindsight . . . The calculus of reasonableness must embody allowance for the fact that police officers are often forced to make split-second judgments about the amount of force that is necessary in a particular situation in circumstances that are tense, uncertain, and rapidly evolving.[97]

In situations that often mirror those encountered by civilian law enforcement, soldiers must be able to make split-second deadly force decisions. Despite this tactical reality, they often are exposed to unnecessary and ill-advised legal and operational scrutiny.

CHAPTER TWELVE

Keeping the United States Out of the International Criminal Court

> We have no eternal allies and we have no perpetual enemies. Our interests are eternal and perpetual, and those interests it is our duty to follow.
>
> —Lord Palmerston, 1848

Following the September 11, 2001, terrorist attacks that claimed the lives of nearly 3,000 Americans, mostly noncombatants, twenty-one-year old Lance Corporal Sam Damon enlisted in the U.S. Marine Corps out of an overwhelming sense of patriotism. The son of a Vietnam War veteran, his ancestors had fought in almost every major American conflict since his great grandfather arrived at Ellis Island from Austria in 1891. Risking their lives for the United States, the Constitution, and their fellow citizens was a matter of honor for the men of the Damon family. They had no idea, however, that within ten years young Sam Damon would be fighting for his liberty as a pawn being sacrificed in the name of globalism before the international community. Having performed his duty with diligence and valor in the mountains of Afghanistan in the years 2008–2009, he faced prosecution years later in an International Criminal Court for the crime of aggression.[98]

This fictional account should bring chills to the hearts of all American service members and their families. Yet despite such a disturbing possibility, many lawyers, scholars, and policy makers continue to march the United States down the road to full membership in the International Criminal Court (ICC). This chapter explores from both legal and strategic perspectives the darker sides of such a trek by examining three important points that make joining the ICC irreconcilable with our constitutionally based republican form of government. They are constitutionally protected individual rights, the American legal notion of the individual right of self-defense, and the influence of Sharia law.

The Strategic Perspective of Lawfare

When you look at any rational strategy formulation model it is important to recognize the tension between global interests and the core values and national interests of the United States. To the peril of America's national interests and, ultimately, her core values, the legal discussion and concomitant risk assessment concerning this issue are monopolized by those favoring a globalist's approach.

If the United States is to retain both its primacy and core constitutional principles, it must flatly reject the call for "a law more readily seen as the reflection of a collective juridical conscience and as a response to the social necessities of States organized as a community."[99] When it comes to defending its core values and beliefs, it must similarly reject the notions of former UN Secretary General Kofi Annan who stated:

> State sovereignty, in its most basic sense, is being redefined—not least by the forces of globalization and international cooperation. States are now widely understood to be instruments at the service of their peoples, and not vice versa.[100]

On certain matters, such as international protocols on freedom of navigation or protection of intellectual property rights, international law helps foster free trade and collective prosperity. On other issues, where agreements would fundamentally undermine the principles and protections of our Constitution, the United States may have to simply agree to disagree with the international community.

This issue is important to strategic leaders now more than ever due to the increasing demands brought about by both the positive and negative effects of globalization. In a project called "Seven Revolutions," the Global Strategy Institute at the Center for Strategic and International Studies (CSIS) identified and analyzed the key policy challenges that policy makers, business figures, and other leaders will face to the year 2025. In an effort to promote strategic thinking on the long-term trends that too few leaders take the time to consider, CSIS identified seven areas of change it expects to be most revolutionary and relevant:

- Population
- Resource management and environmental stewardship
- Technological innovation and diffusion
- The development and dissemination of information and knowledge
- Economic integration
- The nature and mode of conflict
- The challenge of governance[101]

It is this last area—the challenge of governance—that tempts many policy makers and lawyers to militate for a stronger international rule of law. Moreover, those so inclined often see traditional Westphalian nation-states as impediments to the management and development of future global governance. While the future problems identified by CSIS can be positively affected by an international legal structure focused on free trade, commerce, and other communal problems, efforts to expand the authority of international law over the individual should be vigorously resisted.

A number of military judge advocates and legal scholars have taken up the internationalists' call by wrongly believing that international law (as defined by the collective states) demands obeisance and trumps allegiance to our Constitution and country.

> The ICC should be seen as an integral part of the current globalizing tendency in which nations seek to exercise their sovereignty not unilaterally but through cooperative arrangements and rules. This also includes rules to stimulate and regulate the global economy, protect the environment, control the proliferation of weapons of mass destruction, and curb international criminal activity. The United States has long been a leading exponent, and will be a prime beneficiary, of this growing international framework of cooperation.[102]

There is a certain seductive and glamorous element to rubbing elbows with diverse intellectuals from near and afar:

> After 37 years of practicing public international law in general, and dealing with the law of war in particular, I have had the opportunity to form close working relationships with numerous foreign colleagues. In meeting with these individuals in international forums post-9/11, the following scenario has become all too familiar. Spying me across the room, they rush forward— spilling coffee and tea in the process—and exclaim: "What are you people doing? What are you Americans thinking?"[103]

But one must never lose sight of the fact that our system of government, as a constitutional republic, is the sine qua non of why we fight. As so eloquently stated by William F. Buckley Jr., "Materialistic democracy beckons every man to make himself a king; republican citizenship incites every man to be a knight."[104] Therefore, it may first behoove all military officers to recall their simple oath of office:

> I, do solemnly swear (or affirm) that I will support and defend the Constitution of the United States against all enemies, foreign or domestic, that I will bear true faith and allegiance to the same; that I take this obligation freely, without any mental reservations or purpose of evasion; and that I will well and faithfully discharge the duties of the office upon which I am about to enter; So help me God.[105]

This oath, as opposed to the enlisted oath, does not swear to "obey the orders of the President of the United States, the orders of the officers appointed over me, according to regulations and the Uniform Code of Military Justice." There remains only the obligation to defend the Constitution against all enemies, foreign and domestic.

Accordingly, when striving to craft, direct, or influence policy or strategy, a collective, universal rule of law should not be the ultimate goal. This is especially true when the agreed upon universal rule would diminish constitutionally based protections of any American, especially our service members.

By examining the United States' commitment to the ICC in light of three specific areas—constitutionally protected individual rights, the American legal notion of the individual right of self-defense, and the influence of Sharia law—we can more clearly observe the diminution of America's constitutionally derived values. Such a diminution creates an unacceptable fracture of the very social contract—the Constitution—that binds Americans to their government.

Looking at the ICC construct through the lens of our constitutional republican form of government, one sees a court empowered and steered not by a firm rule of law but rather by a collaborative process indentured to the will of the organization rather than a true rule of law designed to protect the individual. As a constitutional republic, America is based upon the primacy of the individual, not the republic. This is a peculiarly American notion foreign to most other nations, and especially those oligarchies, monarchies, and theocracies comprising the ICC.

Constitutionally Protected Individual Rights

As explained by international law scholar and soldier Michael L. Smidt:

> First, the Constitution grants the sole authority to try U.S. citizens to the federal and state courts. Second, certain Bill of Rights protections will not be present at the ICC. Third, certain procedural and structural protection found in U.S. courts may be absent as well.[106]

In essence, the ICC fails to provide basic Fourth Amendment protections against unlawful searches and seizures[107] and the Sixth Amendment right to a speedy trial.[108] The right of confrontation, also found under the Sixth Amendment, may be drastically impaired due to the ICC's extremely relaxed rules on admitting hearsay evidence. Moreover, there are no procedural safeguards in place to provide those charged in the ICC with adequate and competent representation:

> The promise of international criminal law, however, is being eroded by a failure to recognize that a critical underpinning of this

new legal order must be the rights of defendants and how to institutionalize these rights so that there is equality of arms between the defense and the prosecution.[109]

Depriving America's volunteer warriors of constitutional protections that are routinely extended to even the lowliest of our criminal elements would be tragic. A most chilling scenario for any soldier, sailor, airman, or marine would be to survive a life-and-death struggle of close personal combat only to be caught in the crosshairs of a politically motivated ICC adjudging them not by constitutionally derived standards of reasonableness as enunciated by the Supreme Court of the United States, but rather by whatever expedient criminal law formula is in vogue. For instance, the ICC has yet to define the fourth crime in its statute alongside war crimes, crimes against humanity and genocide: the crime of aggression.

I think I can anticipate what will constitute a crime of "aggression" in the eyes of this Court: it will be a crime when the United States of America takes any military action to defend its national interests, unless the U.S. first seeks and receives the permission of the United Nations.[110]

Aggression, or a crime against peace, has been recognized as an international crime since the post-World War II war crimes trials. However, the crime is controversial and difficult to define. A good working definition is the "planning, preparation, initiation or waging of a war of aggression, or a war in violation of international treaties, agreements or assurances, or participation in a common plan or conspiracy for the accomplishment of any of the foregoing."[111] In Mogadishu, UN military spokesman Major David Stockwell stated, "Everyone on the ground in that vicinity was a combatant, because they meant to do us harm. In an ambush, there are no sidelines and no spectators."[112]

From Marine Lance Corporal Justin Sharratt's exoneration from criminal culpability in the aftermath of the November 19, 2005, killings of alleged noncombatants in Haditha, Iraq (after many in the international community—and even a U.S. Congressman—had already convicted him in the court of public opinion) to the near constant post-shooting assessments occurring in both Iraq and Afghanistan today, America's warriors are already under constant threat of criminal indictment.[113] It is only the American constitutionally based system of justice that protects these warriors from being wrongfully imprisoned for perceived mistakes in judgment. This protection would evaporate under many international law constructs. Why then should the United States expose its uniformed service members (or civilians and contractors) serving overseas to such nebulous legal constructs?

The Individual Right of Self-Defense

To understand the issue of self-defense, you first need to understand the robust protections afforded our warriors by both the Constitution and American case law surrounding the use of force in self-defense. In order to appreciate this inherent right of self-defense as recognized and applied in the American system of justice, it is worth examining its historical roots. Historically, the right of self-defense has been viewed not as a statutory or legal right, but as a divine natural right permanently bestowed upon all persons by virtue of existence.

Such constitutional protections and values are at odds with an internationalist's view of the world order and role of governance. One need only look at the invasive European Union rules to see such displays of bureaucratic intrusiveness:

> There is the banning of local Punch and Judy shows in case they encourage domestic violence; insulting committee chairmen by labeling them "chair"—a piece of furniture; changing words like "man" or "black" in case they cause offence; banning competitive sports days so that there are no winners or losers and stopping parents taking photographs of their children in case they are thought to be paedophiles.[114]

As a nation, the United States may bend its principles by treaty to effect a perceived economic gain. However, on such fundamental concerns as self-defense, America must never submit to the will of the collective international masses when discerning what constitutes a justifiable act of self-defense. Again, this is because collective thought often reflects collective ignorance as evidenced by the restrictions imposed by the United Nations on its forces in the Democratic Republic of Congo.

One need not travel to the hinterlands of the Dark Continent to find such anomalies in the international community. In 1993, in Northern Ireland's Belfast Crown Court—in the heart of English common law—British Paratrooper Lance Corporal Lee Clegg was convicted of murdering a passenger in a stolen vehicle driven by his friend at a high rate of speed through a British Army checkpoint. Clegg was serving with the Parachute Regiment's 3rd Battalion when he and other members of a fourteen-man army patrol fired at the car after warnings to stop were ignored. Clegg fired a total of four shots at the car after he believed the vehicle presented an imminent threat of death or serious bodily injury to himself or innocent others. The trial court found that three of the four bullets Clegg fired were justifiable, because he thought the car was being driven at a colleague, but convicted him because the fourth shot was fired when the vehicle had gone past the patrol.

Eventually, Clegg was cleared on appeal:

> The period of time which separated the firing of the first three shots from the fourth (if it was fired into the side of the car) was minimal. The circumstances in which the final shot was fired could not be divorced from the other shots. This is true, in my opinion, whether the last shot was fired at the side or at the rear of the car. The motivation of the accused in firing the fourth shot cannot realistically be segregated from what happened immediately before it.[115]

But not before he spent time in prison as a convicted felon. Had Clegg, like Lance Corporal Justin Sharratt, had the benefit of the American constitutional protections and rule of law, such folly and heartache could have been avoided.

One needs only to look to the activities of the United Nations with respect to gun control and the individual right of self-defense to see collective positivism run amok. A sub-commission of the United Nations Human Rights Council (HRC) has declared that there is "no human right to personal self-defense and that extremely strict gun control is a human right which all governments are required to enforce immediately."[116] This declaration implements a report for the HRC prepared by Special Rapporteur Barbara Frey. In the *BYU Journal of Public Law*, David B. Kopel, Paul Galant, and Joanne D. Eisen comment on the Frey Report:

> Frey's attempt to deny the existence of a human right to self-defense has terrifying implications, which run far beyond her narrow effort to assist international gun prohibition. If Frey is right—that there is no human right to self-defense—then Grotius, Pufendorf, Vattel, Victoria, and all the rest of the humanitarian founders of international law are wrong.
>
> And these humanitarians would not be wrong about an incidental matter (such as whether consuls have the same rights as ambassadors); they would be wrong in the very foundation of their humanitarian principles. The personal right of self-defense is the foundation of the humanitarian edifice built by the classic authors. The personal right to self-defense is why the Indians had a right to resist Spanish pillaging. It is why prisoners of war must be treated humanely, why armies must not target non-combatants, and why aggressive war is unjust.
>
> If Frey is correct that self-defense is not a fundamental human right, then the structure of more than five centuries of humanitarian international law collapses. All the generals, admirals, and diplomats who restrained the conduct of their militaries because they believed in the international law taught by Grotius and the rest were fools, because Grotius and his fellows were concocting international law on the basis of a human right that does not really exist; they were as misguided as the chemists who believed in phlogiston.[117]

Unfortunately, more and more of America's strategic leaders seem to have fallen under the spell of the UN's definitions of what constitutes legitimate international law constructs. To them, all powers flow from and are granted by the state instead of any fundamental God-given right of the individual. Such constructs fly in the face of the United States Constitution and all its source documents.

Influence of Sharia Law

When speaking of the U.S. Supreme Court, Noah Feldman cogently noted:

> In these all-important processes, as always in the history of the court, people are everything. Justices vary widely in temperament, ideology, intelligence and preparedness. The best justices can be really very impressive; the worst ones truly disastrous.[118]

Compared to the potential ills brought upon American society by an imprudent nomination to the Supreme Court, one could safely treble the potential for damage wrought upon the world by an ICC comprised of a conglomeration of judges assembled according to its charter. Article 36 of the ICC states, *inter alia*, that the selection of judges take into account the need for the representation of the principal legal systems of the world and equitable geographical representation. With the global Muslim population standing at 1.57 billion, meaning that nearly 1 in 4 people in the world practice Islam, the influence and impact of Sharia law on such a court must not be ignored.[119]

Legal scholar Alan Dershowitz shows the impact of Sharia law on the world's rule of law when commenting on an incident that transpired in September 2009:

> Last week, Israeli Defense Minister Ehud Barak—the former Dovish Prime Minister who offered the Palestinians a state on all of the Gaza Strip, 95% of the West Bank and a capital in East Jerusalem—was arrested when he set foot in Great Britain. (He was quickly released on grounds of diplomatic immunity because he was an official visitor.) And now Moshe Yaalon, an Israeli government minister and former Army Chief of Staff, was forced to cancel a trip he was scheduled to make in London on behalf of a charity, for fear that he too would be arrested.
>
> The charges against these two distinguished public officials are that they committed war crimes against Palestinian terrorists and civilians. Yaalon was accused in connection with the 2002 targeted killing of Salah Shehadeh, a notorious terrorist who was responsible for the deaths of hundreds of Israeli civilians and was

planning the murders of hundreds of more. As a result of faulty intelligence the rocket that killed Shehadeh also killed several civilians who were nearby, including members of his own family. Barak is being accused of war crimes in connection with Israel's recent military effort to stop rockets from being fired at its civilians from the Gaza Strip.[120]

By way of this real world example, you can see that it is not a specious stretch to assert that politics will trump the rule of law in many instances. Nor is it inconceivable to envision how the rule of law as applied by the ICC will be used by groups applying legal constructs not only foreign to but fundamentally at odds with the principles enunciated by the Founding Fathers.

You don't need to go to radical or extremist jihadi websites to find potential for conflict between the rule of law as practiced by Western civilization and that set forth in Islamic society. From the English language translation of the Saudi-published *Interpretation of the Meanings of the Noble Qur'an in the English Language*, one can read that *jihad*—holy fighting in Allah's Cause—is a requirement of Islam:

> The Verses of the Qur'an and the *Sunnah* (*the* Prophet's legal ways, orders) exhort Muslims greatly to take part in *Jihad* and have made quite clear its rewards, and praised greatly those who perform *Jihad* (the holy fighting in Allah's Cause) and explained to them various kinds of honours which they will receive from their Lord (Allah). This is because they—*mujahidin*—are Allah's troops. Allah will establish His religion (Islam), through them (*mujahidin*). He will repel the might of His enemies, and through them He will protect Islam and guard the religion safely. And it is they (*mujahidin*) who fight against the enemies of Allah in order that the worship should be all for Allah (Alone and not for any other deity) and that the Word of Allah (i.e. none has the right to be worshipped but Allah and His religion Islam) should be superior.[121]

The 1990 Cairo Declaration—the "Universal Declaration of Human Rights in Islam"—was drafted and subsequently ratified by all the Muslim member nations of the Organization of the Islamic Conference (OIC). This declaration was an Islamic response to the post-World War II United Nations' Universal Declaration of Human Rights (UDHR) of 1948. The OIC represents the entire Muslim Ummah (or global community of individual Muslims) and is the largest single voting bloc in the United Nations. According to its own website, "the Organization of the Islamic Conference (OIC) is the second largest inter-governmental organization after the United Nations which has membership of 57 states spread over four continents. The Organization is the collective voice of the Muslim world and ensuring to safeguard and protect the interests of the Muslim world in the spirit of promoting international peace and harmony among various people of the world."[122]

Both the preamble and concluding articles of the Cairo Declaration make plain that it is designed to supersede Western conceptions of human rights as enunciated in diverse bodies of law such as the U.S. Bill of Rights and the UN's 1948 Universal Declaration of Human Rights. From the Cairo Declaration on Human Rights in Islam, adopted and issued at the Nineteenth Islamic Conference of Foreign Ministers in Cairo on August 5, 1990: "Reaffirming the civilizing and historical role of the Islamic Ummah which God made the best nation that has given mankind a universal and well-balanced civilization in which harmony is established between this life and the hereafter and knowledge is combined with faith; and the role that this Ummah should play to guide a humanity confused by competing trends and ideologies and to provide solutions to the chronic problems of this materialistic civilization."[123]

The opening of the preamble to the Cairo Declaration repeats a Quranic injunction affirming Islamic supremacies, (Quran 3:110; "You are the *best nation* ever brought forth to men . . . you believe in *Allah*"), and states, "Reaffirming the civilizing and historical role of the Islamic Ummah *which Allah made the best nation . . .*"[124]

The preamble continues,

"Believing that fundamental rights and universal freedoms in Islam are an integral part of the Islamic religion and that no one as a matter of principle has the right to suspend them in whole or in part or violate or ignore them in as much as they are binding divine commandments, which are contained in the Revealed Books of God and were sent through the last of His Prophets to complete the preceding divine messages thereby making their observance an act of worship and their neglect or violation an abominable sin, and accordingly every person is individually responsible—and the Ummah collectively responsible—for their safeguard."[125]

The Cairo Declaration also maintains that "all the rights and freedoms stipulated in this Declaration are subject to the Islamic Shari'a" that "the Islamic Shari'a is the *only* source of reference for the explanation or clarification to any of the articles of this Declaration."[126]

The Cairo Declaration's reference to the Ummah is not generally understood by Western tradition:

> A concept that has no real equivalent in the West, discussions of the *Ummah* in Islamic terms ends up seeming too opaque to most Western sensibilities. Either way, decision makers and analysts are prone to discount Islamic concepts they do not understand by characterizing them in cultural mythology or utopian terms. As with the associated concept of the caliphate, the *Ummah* is a currently existing reality given specific definition in Islamic law and reflected in the national constitutions of the Muslim countries surveyed. In terms of either the greater Arab Nation or the Muslim *Ummah*, one needs look no further than currently existing *Ummah*-level organizations like the Arab League, the Supreme Islamic Counsel, the Organization of the Islamic Conference (OIC) or the Muslim World League—all of which have demonstrated an ability to speak with authority.[127]

At the core of the radical front of Islam, the hard-core elite of al Qaeda and the Muslim Brotherhood recognize the irreconcilability of Islam with a constitutional republic. Sayyid Qutb, the father of the Muslim Brotherhood, wrote a thirty-volume commentary on the Quran, later condensed to a short manifesto called *Milestones Along the Way*. In it Qutb expounds that the entire Islamic world had left true Islam, and that he and his cobelievers were the only ones who understood Islam. He felt the target of the struggle should be the United States and Britain, whose notions of democracy directly contradicted his definition of *tawhid*, the Islamic notion of the supremacy and oneness of God. Interestingly, Qutb was among those executed in one of Egyptian President Nasser's crackdowns in the 1960s, but his brother Mohammed Qutb fled to Saudi Arabia and became a university teacher; among his pupils was Osama bin Laden.[128]

If the United States willingly enters into the legal corpus or sphere with the global community, it should recognize that the other parties to the agreement will not be playing with the same spirit of ecumenism. While some would argue that we should join the ICC in order to be able to shape it, the cold reality may be that certain strongly held beliefs within the global community are simply incompatible with the development and implementation of one corpus of law. Elements of Sharia law provide a shining example of such incompatibility.

American exceptionalism is only as dead as America allows it to become. Alexis de Tocqueville's acknowledgment that the United States holds a special place among nations was fundamentally predicated upon its constitutional precepts that allowed for a country of diverse immigrants to thrive under a democratic republic. Diminishing or ceding such values solely to achieve international consensus for consensus' sake is not in America's collective or individual best interest. Doing so also ignores the sage warning of Walter Lippman: "A policy is bound to fail which deliberately violates our pledges and our principles, our treaties and our laws. The American conscience is a reality."[129] The Senate may cede certain sovereign immunities when ratifying treaties with foreign governments, but it should not cede the constitutional liberties and protections of our individual citizens, especially those who volunteer to fight in far-off lands.

More important, ceding such liberties and protections severely undermines our domestic social contract as set forth in the Constitution. In other words, the Constitution is more than mere statutory language. It is a unique social contract between a people and their government that defines the concept of a servant state as opposed to a served state. In other words, citizens of a constitutional republic should be served by a minimalist government that is only as large as it needs to be. Compare this to a European socialist state that is served by its subjects in furtherance of the state's interests. Recognizing and protecting this distinction from further diminution in the name of globalism is critical to America's survival as a constitutional republic.

We should not expose our young soldiers to the prospect of being hauled before a hostile, politically inspired international court to answer allegations that they broke nebulously defined crimes. This is especially true if our warriors would have to proceed in a system absent the full protections of our constitutionally guaranteed rights, to include the right to trial by jury. Yet this is exactly the road down which the internationalists want America to travel. Unfortunately, to some degree, the internationalists have invaded our military and its Judge Advocate General's Corps.

This violation of our social contract was also reflected in the troubling Department of Homeland Security (DHS) report of April 7, 2009, which warned against the possibility of violence by unnamed "right-wing extremists" concerned about illegal immigration, increasing federal power, restrictions on firearms, abortion, and the loss of U.S. sovereignty, and that singles out returning war veterans as particular threats to the United States they so willingly and courageously defended. Furthermore, at a hearing on Muslim radicalization in U.S. prisons in June of this year, Representative Sheila Jackson Lee tried to derail the hearings by insisting that "investigators needed to analyze Christian militants in America because they too might try to bring down the country." Not too many Christians have been running around shooting people and blowing themselves up in the name of Christianity.

The report only validates the fears of many Americans, especially those of us "clinging to our religion and guns," to borrow President Obama's phrase. Former Chief of Staff Rahm Emanuel's quote that "You never let a serious crisis go to waste. And what I mean by that is it's an opportunity to do things you could not do before" should be placed in proper historical context. Proud, law-abiding Americans should be concerned that the current administration will use "every contingency to strengthen itself" (heeding John Adams's words of warning about a government's nature to grow if unchecked). That the DHS report willfully ignores the real threats and unnecessarily targets those who don't subscribe to the neo-socialist views of the ruling party provides insight into its authors' disregard of the constitutionally defined social contract. In essence, the authors of the report attempt to define and target folks here in America based upon their contrary, but constitutional, political beliefs rather than obvious indicia of dangerousness like connections to radical Islamic mullahs and overt statements about the supremacy of Islam.

DHS's labeling as "extremists" those citizens who: believe in the Second Amendment; are concerned about the seemingly uncontrolled growth and influence of the federal government; and, oppose abortion and transnationalism is an abuse of power of the highest order. Under DHS's rubric, a veteran of Iraq and Afghanistan who is also a member of the National Rifle Association and believes, like Ronald Reagan, that less government is better government, must be a prime suspect.

Second, to single out American service members who have served in Iraq or Afghanistan—sometimes for three and four back-to-back tours—as a heightened threat ignores the patriotism, valor, and love of country these men and women possess. Those men and women—unlike Major Nidal Hasan, who had never deployed—that willingly risked their lives in Iraq and Afghanistan are the *least* likely to harm their fellow citizens and America. The bureaucrats and elitists may not understand this, but those who serve certainly do.

It is the long-term threat to America that such insidious reports pose that is of most concern. Decent hardworking Americans have steadily watched the erosion of our social contract, the free market economy, as well as our individual rights and liberties, by an ever-growing and influential federal government. Paraphrasing Robert Bork, we have been "slouching toward Gomorrah" for decades. It is time for this to end: Most Americans serving in uniform understand their oath and allegiance to the Constitution and are prepared to defend it against all enemies, foreign and domestic.

CHAPTER THIRTEEN

Some Solutions

Amerca's military needs to be a martial entity near-singularly focused on what it should be prepared to do: defend the United States by force against all enemies, foreign and domestic. It should not continue its march down the VUCA-defined road toward peacekeeping, nation-building, and COIN missions. The threats on the horizon, to include the continued global growth of the Islamists and the threats of traditional nation-states like China, Russia, Iran, and North Korea, will require our focused attention to remain competitive on land, sea, air, space, and cyberspace. The following are some policy recommendations on how we can regain lost martial virtues and hone the tip of our nation's spear.

For fear of retribution or marginalization, no one is forcing the debate in the areas of concern set forth herein. The following thoughts and recommendations are designed to foment discussion and debate. They will, no doubt, cause anger and angst in some readers. Rigorous thought, as well as critical and creative thinking, should be frank, painful, and brutally honest.

Define America's Go-to-War Doctrine and Stop Violating the Sovereignty of Nations

Our policy makers, whether political or senior military, are too tempted to use the only element of national power, the military, which has the capacity to perform missions better left to other elements of power. We have seen this in Iraq and Afghanistan and on too many other occasions. We consistently use the military to perform missions better suited to the Department of State, or for that matter the Peace Corps. Moreover, if you use blunt instruments for precision surgery, don't be surprised at the resulting trauma to the body. Because of the focused, can-do spirit and personality of the military command and staff tasked with such unmilitary missions, instead of questioning the propriety of using the military in such fashions, these good and dedicated people finesse the mission with a full-court press.

When senior military leaders provide guidance to their senior service schools, it is often in the form of "create imaginative and critical thinkers."[130] To this end, the diverse service schools churn out creative officers who, unfortunately, seem only to focus upon predetermined missions and tasks given them such as COIN and nation-building missions. Instead, these creative types should be encouraged to question and consider the appropriate roles and missions for our armed forces. It is at this level that all the teachings of Sun Tzu and Clausewitz become most relevant, not at the operational or tactical level of war.

Confusing and obfuscating this inquiry and discussion, the diverse departments and agencies within the government, including the Department of Defense, seek ways to increase their budgets and end-strength. Add to this avaricious stew the malignant influence of many, many defense contractors who would like nothing more than the expansion of Department of Defense's roles and missions. For instance, in many large agencies and sub-agencies, like JIEDDO, there exists the untenable situation where contractors, whose fiduciary duties lie with their parent company, are in positions to write and otherwise influence contractual requirements for the government. In other words, contractors are having direct and indirect influence on the government's decision to scope and award contracts. Truly the fox is watching the henhouse. This situation exists for many reasons, not the least of which is the government's attempts to save money by not hiring enough governmental workers to fill its operational billets—operational billets required, in part, due to the misuse and overuse of the military throughout the world. The A-76 initiative, tantamount to a decision to transfer agency work from public employees directly accountable to the agency to a private or public entity accountable only to the sometimes nebulous terms of the contract, is one example of this unfettered and out-of-control feed trough.

Using the military for such non-military roles has, in turn, increased the political clout and budget of our Department of Defense, which in turn causes further expansion of its mission responsibilities. Also, other agencies, such as the Department of State, have no outside lobbyists badgering for increases in their strength.

Thus the first and most obvious adjustment begins at the strategic or policy level: Stop using military elements of national power in halfhearted and misguided efforts to coerce change in the internal working of sovereign states. The United States, as a unilateral superpower, would be better off fiscally and be less vulnerable to attack if it followed the guidance of George Washington in his farewell address:

> The nation which indulges towards another a habitual hatred or a habitual fondness is in some degree a slave. It is a slave to its animosity or to its affection, either of which is sufficient to lead it astray from its duty and its interest. Antipathy in one nation against another disposes each more readily to offer insult and injury, to lay hold of slight causes of umbrage, and to be haughty and intractable, when accidental or trifling occasions of dispute occur . . . So likewise, a passionate attachment of one nation for another produces a variety of evils. Sympathy for the favorite nation, facilitating the illusion of an imaginary common interest in cases where no real common interest exists, and infusing into one the enmities of the other, betrays the former into a participation in the quarrels and wars of the latter without adequate inducement or justification.[131]

Why should the United States care if Afghanistan is run by a Taliban-like oligarchy or a loose confederation of thirty-seven different tribal warlords? Or if Iraq, Pakistan, or any other Muslim state governs itself under Sharia law? Or if women are treated differently than they are in the West? It is none of our business.

The elites believe that "human rights law" trumps a nation's sovereignty and its ability to defend itself. It gives the benefit of the doubt to the bad guys and allows the good to be victimized with no alternatives. It is axiomatic that they also believe a soldier's individual rights to self-defense can be limited.

But such a liberal globalized vision runs smack up against two very obstinate and formidable barriers: our Constitution here in America and the faith of the Ummah in the Muslim lands. There may come a time when those two barriers become diametrically opposed in a worldwide crusade—or true clash of civilizations[132]—but the best solution for the foreseeable future would be for the West to retrench and strengthen itself domestically and within its spheres of influence and interact with foreign nations on purely economic and trade bases as does China. Why would it be so difficult for us to do so as well? We can maintain the freedom of the commons with our strong navy and trade with Muslim nations in the marketplace of commodities, not ideologies.

If the United States wishes to become involved in the internal affairs of other nations, it should do so only by invitation and only when it involves a vital national interest. The military should not take the lead unless there is a legitimate military target and objective. Otherwise the United States should strengthen and use its foreign policy advisory teams at other government agencies like the Department of State or USAID to strengthen its economic and diplomatic position around the globe. At the moment, the Department of State budget is overwhelmingly dwarfed by the Department of Defense's. And if all one has is a hammer, most problems tend to look like a nail. Unfortunately, in attempting to solve un-nail-like problems, the Department of Defense is gradually morphing into something other than a hammer.

Thus, strategic leaders, and congress if necessary, should insist on the immediate strengthening of manpower, material, and budget of those agencies within the government that should take the lead on foreign affairs issues. Imagine instead of our government turning to the Defense Intelligence Agency (DIA) for information about another nation's economy, it turns instead to the State Department or the Department of Treasury.

Clarify the Chairman Joint Chiefs of Staff's SROE

To those familiar with its history and command intent, the current SROE (Standing Rules of Engagement) provides plenty of authority for soldiers, sailors, airmen, and marines to use deadly force in self-defense. Problems arise, however, when layers of subordinate commands and their judge advocates negatively impact that authority by not training their warriors in threat identification and response and watering down the language in misguided attempts to prevent collateral civilian damage and deaths. More disturbing is that a number of judge advocates continue to opine—wrongly—that the current SROE does not recognize the individual inherent right to self-defense. Such opinions derive from unclear language in Para.3.a of the current rule:

Inherent Right of Self-Defense.

Unit Commanders always retain the inherent right and obligation to exercise unit self-defense in response to a hostile act or demonstrated hostile intent. *Unless otherwise directed by a unit commander as directed below*, military members may exercise self-defense in response to a hostile act or demonstrated hostile intent. (Emphasis added.)

The exception—unless otherwise directed by a unit commander as directed below—concerns situations where a commander, for purposes of unit or collective self-defense, can override an individual's notions of what is a reasonable response to a perceived threat. This language was added at the insistence of the navy, which had concerns over command and control of its larger weapons systems. It has nothing to do with and in no way limits the inherent *individual* right of self-defense in close-in combat situations. This is simply a matter of interpreting statutory construction: The exception does not become the rule. Yet some judge advocates, perhaps in an attempt to "empower" their commanders or limit collateral damage, continue to opine otherwise.

A rewrite of the SROE would fix these problems. At a minimum the new SROE, in relevant part, should say the following:

Soldiers, sailors, airmen, and marines may use deadly force in self-defense when confronted with imminent threat of death or serious bodily injury to self or innocent others. If deadly force is used in self-defense in the line of duty, service members will not be judged in the clear vision of 20/20 hindsight but rather how a reasonable soldier, sailor, airman, or marine would act under situations that are tense, uncertain, and rapidly evolving.

Commanders at all levels of command have the responsibility to train their forces on the threats extant in their area of operations as well as on relevant pre-assaultive behaviors that may reasonably signal such threats. Commanders shall provide all personnel the means and ability to use the appropriate amount of force to quell any such threat.

No subordinate commander can limit this inherent individual right of a service member when that service member is in close contact with an enemy or threat.

This language should apply both overseas as well as here in the United States. It would provide the command support necessary for protecting our soldiers in combat situations as well as in garrison. Moreover it would demand that proper training be emplaced to provide our warriors with the skills and abilities to properly discern and quell authentic threats. There is always limited "white space" or free time in unit training calendars. But more thought should be given to mandatory tactical training instead of mandatory EO or Information Awareness (IA) training. Also if leadership does not take time to tactically train, they should not try to control possible bad outcomes with more restrictive ROE! To do so is a dereliction of duty and a sign of moral cowardice. Senior leaders should make decisions based on the premise that "American lives are inherently more valuable than our adversaries." If not, why do we fight?

Better Training and Command Support for Troops' Use of Force

If one were to ask the average soldier, sailor, airman, or marine how often he used a computer keyboard in the performance of his duty or privately, the answer would be on a near-daily basis. Consequently such an individual would be intimate with the functioning of that keyboard: never needing to look to find the space bar or shift key. On the other hand, if one were to ask the average soldier, sailor, airman, or marine to manipulate the selector switch on his M-4 or M-9 weapon, most would have to look to do so. This is because the military—except for select units—does not encourage intimacy with the primary tool in each service member's toolkit: the individual weapon. Instead, the military focuses upon "weapons qualification" and safety. Qualification courses, while fine for demonstrating an ability of the weapon to actually hit a stationary target that is not firing back, lend very little utility to one's ability to fight and win in combat. It is merely a liability reducer, not a lifesaver. Qualification is *not* training, and training is *not* qualification. This is a subtle—yet key—distinction that commanders must grasp. Moreover there is precious little instruction given to the average soldier on how to identify and react to an imminent threat of death or serious bodily injury. On the contrary, soldiers learn from Escalation of Force (EOF) cards how not to engage. An example of such a dangerous and nearly useless EOF card is shown on the following page.

Such linear flowchart guidance may look good at a commander's PowerPoint morning briefing, but it is horrific legal and tactical guidance for a soldier at the tip of the spear. It neither respects the laws of physics as they relate to time-distance factors nor takes into consideration the physiological realities of action versus reaction. Legally, its only utility is to paint a soldier into a no-win corner when used to assess behavior during a post-shooting investigation. Unfortunately, PowerPoint briefings have become the norm for the military. They have replaced sound judgment and the ability to communicate orally and to physically lead. Little cutting-edge or critical thinking now occurs because senior leaders demand everything on a "Quad Chart" briefing so they can assess metrics rather than sound thought. The military has swallowed hook, line, and sinker the "Lean Six Sigma" management style of Toyota to the exclusion of true leadership and critical thinking.

The practical problem with such linear-based thinking is that at the tactical level it fails to account for simple physics. If a vehicle is approaching a checkpoint at a mere 30 miles per hour, that speed translates into 44 feet per second, so if a soldier perceives that a vehicle a block away is a potential threat, he will only have a few seconds to observe, discern, decide what action to take, and then act. The brain does not work all that well under stress. This reality is considered in the next section.

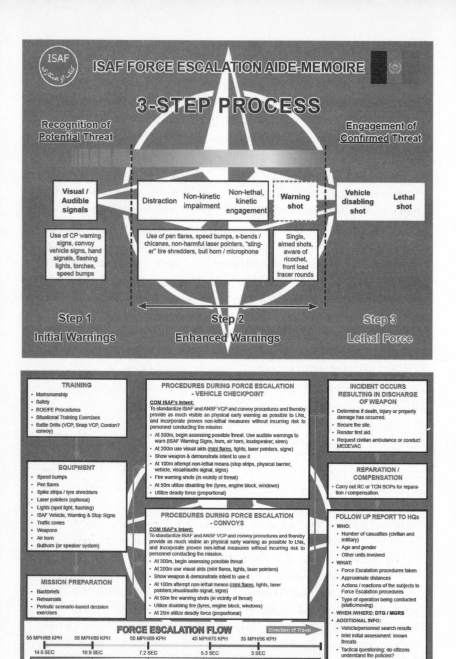

ISAF Escalation of Force Cards, circa 2009.

Judgment-based Engagement Training (JET) Seminar

In 2000, a group of judge advocates and tactical weapons instructors collaborated to develop the Rules of Engagement (ROE)/Rules for Use of Force (RUF) Tactical Training Seminar.[133] This seminar concept derived from groundbreaking work initiated by ROE and RUF experts W. Hays Parks (DoD) and John C. Hall (FBI). Since then, this course has been taught using a mobile training team to thousands of students in organizations ranging from Special Operations Command Central and 1st Armored Training Brigade to Naval Expeditionary Combat Command and the Defense Institute for International Legal Studies. It has, over time, been renamed the Judgment-based Engagement Training (JET) Seminar.[134] JET is an acronym first developed by Captain Mark Kohart, USN, and Commander Thomas Mowell, USN, at the Navy Center for Security Forces in Little Creek, Virginia, after they successfully integrated the ROE/RUF Tactical Training Seminar concept into their program of instruction for deploying naval forces performing in-lieu-of mission in Iraq and Afghanistan.

The program of instruction effectively trains military members, commanders, and their judge advocates concerning lawful and tactically sound application of the use of deadly force. The judgment-based training curriculum is the opposite of the usual rules-based training and offers realistic situational and firearms instruction beyond that rendered by traditional lectures, lane exercises, and marksmanship range training done in isolation from one another. Further, such judgment-based training enhances traditional force-on-force combat skills. And it is unique, innovative, and essential for the missions faced in the post-9/11 world.

These seminars—generally two to three days long—provide a detailed overview of the law and the tactical dynamics of deadly force encounters: action versus reaction, Tache-Psyche Effect (the psycho-physiological reactions of humans under high-stress tactical environments), and wound ballistics. Expert instructors from various military departments, law enforcement agencies, civilian experts, and legal instructors provide the classroom instruction. Later, students viscerally experience the phenomena and issues discussed in the classroom by using diverse situational training exercises and devices, including: Engagement Skills Trainer, Firearms

Training System, non-lethal marking rounds, and live-fire judgment-based targets on the range.

Such force-on-force training creates a level of "stress inoculation" against some of the more deadly aspects of fear and stress-induced physiological and psychological effects. The program provides the operators with essential information regarding the use of force along with holistic knowledge and practical applications. Throughout both the dynamic and interactive training regimens, students are forced to rely upon near-instantaneous judgment—judgment that can only be honed by exposure to a variety of complex situations requiring immediate detection, decision, and reaction. Increased understanding of tactical threats cultivates judgment through the fluid integration of decision-making and tactical concerns. Very simply, confidence in use of force authority and skill leads to operator competence and increases the likelihood of killing more bad guys and potentially fewer civilians.

Apart from conflicts where America's national leadership has declared a force or group to be "hostile" or designated them as "enemy combatants," soldiers, sailors, airmen, and marines will always be responding to a hostile act or demonstrated hostile intent much as police officers do on a daily basis in the United States. Moreover, even when a group like al Qaeda has been declared hostile, they don't wear al Qaeda T-shirts or distinctive uniforms, so we are nearly always responding in a self-defense mode because the bad guys attack first. Accordingly our service members need to be educated on threat identification or else face getting shot in the face before even recognizing that a threat exists.

Soldiers are not born with an ability to discern between friend and foe. Many lessons learned from law enforcement concerning threat identification must be incorporated into the military's training regimen. The first lesson is a psychological one: Human beings rarely, if ever, expect something bad to happen to them. It is always the other guy who gets into a car accident, the other family's home that is burglarized, and always the other convoys that get hit by the IED. If we were expecting to get into a gunfight, would we not bring something bigger than a pistol or rifle? It is almost a universal reaction of surprise that greets most warriors and cops when they become involved in a deadly force encounter, even when responding to armed holdup calls and calls where, intellectually, the officers should have known a violent encounter was likely.

While teaching the JET seminar at the United States Air Force Expeditionary Center in December 2005, the team was approached by an army master sergeant assigned to the Warrior Brigade, U.S. Army Civil Affairs and Psychological Operations Command (USACAPOC), Fort Bragg, North Carolina. In his civilian life, this soldier was a police officer in Arkansas. He told the team, and then the class, of his ordeal of confronting two violent, armed robbers at a convenience store. Rolling into the store parking lot, he saw two armed men running out the front door. His first reaction was one of surprise. As he got out of his car, he was surprised a second time: The two men did not flee. Instead they charged at him with their weapons blazing. The officer's first reaction was one of incredulity: Bad guys were supposed to run when confronted by the police. He quickly recovered his wits, retreated to the back of his vehicle, and then went into his training mode: front site on target/trigger press. He quickly and successfully hit both subjects multiple times. Again to his surprise, only one subject went down immediately, while the second subject hurdled over his downed partner and continued to charge. The officer quickly performed a combat reload (without hesitation and without thinking) and put more rounds into the second bad guy, hitting him with a fatal T shot to the brain. That subject was DRT (dead right there), with his automatic pistol empty and slide locked to the rear. The officer then shifted his attention back to the first downed subject, who—unbelievably to the officer (having hit him with multiple rounds)—was trying to push himself up off the ground to continue the attack. It took more rounds from the officer to finally finish the job of addressing that threat. This event shook the officer profoundly, but he reports that it was the fact that he was twice-surprised during the event that impacted him most. This same type of surprise occurs in urban combat with surprising frequency, so training soldiers on this type of law enforcement example can only help soldiers learn what to expect and how to react. The first time they see a subject survive multiple hits should not be in a life-and-death combat setting.

Also, we are not born preprogrammed with much in the way of threat recognition. Nearly all of what we know is learned rather than innate. For instance, most reasonable adults—without training—would not recognize that an opponent who was "blading" his body into a pre-assaultive stance or balling his fists was showing signals of imminent attack. Yet any reasonably well-trained police officer would commit to a first strike with an

ASP baton on a subject who exhibited such signs of a probable assault during a field interview. Neither prudence nor the law requires the law enforcement officer take the first punch in such a situation. In fact, the officer does not even need "probable cause" (a legal threshold meaning "more likely than not") to believe an assault is imminent. The law only requires "reasonable suspicion" on the officer's part. In other words, the law does not require an officer to gamble with his life, nor is the Constitution a suicide pact. Members of the armed forces do not give up such constitutional protections when they raise their right hand to defend America.

Nevertheless, before an individual can lawfully use deadly force in self-defense or defense of innocent others, one must be confronted with an individual or group that has demonstrated the hostile intent, ability, and opportunity to inflict death or grievous bodily injury upon oneself or innocent others. The law enforcement training model used to instruct on this concept is called the threat triangle:

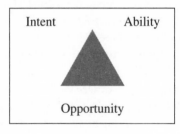

Threat triangle.

We do not need to teach our soldiers, sailors, airmen, and marines clairvoyant maneuvers to divine hostile intent. In fact, a suspect's subjective intent, legally and tactically, is not at all relevant. An insane person, or someone highly intoxicated on drugs or alcohol, may possess very little ability to formulate subjective hostile intent. Or as our friend and mentor John C. Hall is fond of quoting, "Very little mentation is required for deadly action. A rattlesnake is deadly but could not form the mental state required for conviction of murder."

Rather, we should be training our warriors as we train our cops, especially when sending them into uncertain environments where the threats are not wearing enemy uniforms. We should train them to recognize objective hostile intent. Many lessons can be gleaned from the law enforcement experience in identifying such intent, which can be applied to military missions. When using force in self-defense, it is immaterial whether the suspect posing the threat is a hard-core member of al Qaeda or the pizza deliveryman gone berserk.

Individuals (other than when striking from a hidden ambush position) generally do not initiate a violent act without first exhibiting certain pre-assaultive behaviors (or "clues" as they say in law enforcement settings). In other words, a trained law enforcement officer will be attuned to the body language—such as the aforementioned blading of the body or balling of the fists—that often occurs before an offensive action is undertaken by a suspect. Some other pre-assaultive behaviors are anger or determination in the facial mien; pacing, puffing out of the chest; and strutting or bull-like pawing of the earth with one's feet.

Perhaps the most prevalent pre-assaultive behavior threat indicator is verbal noncompliance. If a uniformed, armed police officer (or soldier) is pointing a weapon and yelling "Freeze" or "Halt," compliance is required. Most reasonable people, regardless of whether the verbal warning is in a foreign language, will find it prudent to follow such direction. An individual should not be surprised if he is shot after openly disobeying a cop or soldier who is pointing a weapon and ordering him to freeze or halt. If a suspect starts playing "stupid" (as in "what, me?") or instead ignores the command completely, then that behavior should immediately be seen as a danger sign to the cop or soldier that something bad is about to happen. Under certain circumstances, such as when a suspect ignores a command to "drop the knife" or "keep your hands where I can see them," the verbal noncompliance might be an immediate precursor to deadly force. Under those circumstances, at the very minimum, the verbal noncompliance of a subject should place the officer or soldier in a heightened state of alertness and awareness that something may be awry. Yet in the military we fail to teach these important points. More frighteningly, we continue to hamstring our forces with Escalation of Force rubrics and ill-founded post-shooting investigations.

More than any other part of the human body, the hands of a suspect are constantly a concern for most prudent law enforcement officers. The mouth may be running, or the eyes batting, but it is the hands that will most likely access the weapon or initiate the assault upon the suspect's intended victim. That is why verbal noncompliance by a potentially armed suspect to a command "show me your hands" must be viewed as a sign of demonstrated hostile intent or imminent hostile act. Under such circumstances, officers would be foolhardy to wait to see a weapon before taking immediate action. The same holds true in combat settings, yet very few soldiers are ever taught this lifesaving fact. Many judge advocates and commanders wrongly instruct their warriors to wait until a threat actually points or fires his weapon before deadly force is authorized.

More than one suspect or assailant dramatically increases the danger to a soldier or law enforcement officer. Despite Hollywood movies showing cops (or martial arts experts) fending off two, three, or more attackers, the advantage a group has over an individual is high and the odds are not in favor of the individual no matter how skilled a fighter he may be. This is true even though the officer or soldier may possess the only firearm on the scene. In addition to the sheer physical advantage multiple assailants possess over the individual cop or soldier, multiple assailants are also a danger due to a tunnel vision dynamic that comes into play: In other words, the soldier or cop may be so distracted by an "obvious" bad guy (either an actual or feigned threat) that he will exclude or not focus on other possible threats within the group until it is too late.

Soldiers are often faced with this dilemma at traffic control points and entry control points. That is why it is critical that there be sufficient personnel present, hopefully in an "overwatch" position with a clear field of fire, to attenuate this problem. But out on patrol or conducting peace-enforcing missions, soldiers may not have that luxury. They need to be trained on threat identification and recognize that a hostile crowd—even if apparently unarmed—can still present a very serious threat. If the mission allows, it may be prudent for the patrol to quickly exfiltrate an area to avoid a potentially ugly and uneven situation. But the soldiers have to first be trained on recognizing the problem before seeking solutions.

The previously utilized tactics, techniques, and procedures (TTPs) of the enemy can be a huge building block in the development of assessing hostile intent. If the enemy has been known to use an injured civilian as a ruse to stop a convoy or divert the attention of a patrol, should that situation arise again, the patrol would be wise to go into "condition yellow" quickly; in other words, be really switched on and wary of attack.

Lastly, so long as it is efficiently and accurately pumped down to the lowest tactical levels, theater-specific intelligence can also be used as a building block to divine intent. Law enforcement lawfully and reasonably relies on similar reports all the time. For instance, if a cop receives an "all points bulletin" (APB) or "be on the lookout" for a violent and armed criminal suspect, and then that cop performs a car stop on a vehicle and driver matching the description of that APB, the officer would be smart (and within his legal rights) to treat that situation as a "felony car stop." In other words, the officer should safely remove the individual at gunpoint from the vehicle. If the driver, known to fit the description of an armed and violent felon, disregards the officer's commands, the officer may be prudent to use force on that subject even before ever seeing a weapon, given verbal noncompliance or any other indicator of an incipient attack. The law allows the officer to rely on police communications and intelligence concerning that individual. Similarly, if a soldier possesses threat information gleaned from U.S. or coalition intelligence sources, the soldier should reasonably be able to rely on such information when developing an immediate threat assessment of possible hostile intent. The law does not require the soldier to be "positive," only reasonable. Too often, however, warriors are advised, "You can't shoot unless you have positive ID or PID!" What nonsense, both legally and tactically.

Sadly most civilians (and, it appears, judge advocates) gain their knowledge concerning the ability of an adversary to inflict death or grievous bodily injury from Hollywood. Current rules in many ROE include "use minimum force," "use proportionate force," "exhaust lesser means," or "don't load a round into the chamber until confronted with an imminent threat." A logical extension of this would require a little old lady being attacked by a mugger with a knife to defend herself only with a knife. Proportionate force, however, does not mean "fair" or "equivalent" force. Too many judge advocates and—it seems—commanders deem it to be.

The best example of this misunderstanding can be found when law enforcement officers confront an individual armed with an edged weapon. Most people unskilled or uneducated in such matters become upset when a cop or group of cops shoots a suspect armed only with a knife, and sometimes from seemingly "safe" distances for the police. Immediately the caterwauling from the civil rights groups and media begins. Some ask, "Why didn't the officers 'swarm' the suspect; there were four cops and only one bad guy?" They ignore the obvious question—"Who wants to be the first swarmer?" Such Monday morning quarterbacking ignores the ability of an individual armed with an edged weapon to inflict death or grievous bodily injury on a group thirty feet away armed with firearms before they could effectively mount an effective response. Recall the image from the Indiana Jones movie where Indy shoots dead a scimitar-wielding assailant who only brought a knife to a gunfight. While an effective movie ploy, the scene inaccurately represents the true threat an individual with an edged weapon presents. In a real-world scenario—due to the realities of wound ballistics and the hit-miss ratios—Indy would stand a very good chance of getting cut badly, if not killed, by the assailant.

The realities of wound ballistics, action-versus-reaction, and the fact that law enforcement officers miss approximately 80 percent of the time during actual engagements, will tilt the scales in favor of the assailant. Law enforcement officers are trained on these realities, and that is why prudence and the law allow them to engage. It should never be a fair or proportionate fight. Many judge advocates incorrectly infuse the Law of War principle of proportionality into tactical ROE concerning rules for the use of deadly force. Proportionality in Law of War terms simply means that in military operations force should be proportionate to a threat in order to avoid unnecessary civilian casualties or collateral damage. In other words, it may be imprudent to drop a 2,000-pound bomb in the middle of a crowded marketplace in order to take out one enemy combatant because that may cause disproportionate collateral damage or death to innocents. Proportionality has absolutely nothing to do with how one should respond with small arms to a hostile act or demonstrated hostile intent. Yet too many times ROE/RUF is infused with this concept—"the force used must be proportional to the threat"[135] implying that somehow confrontations with a hostile actor must be "fair."

It is common knowledge among trained law enforcement officers that a suspect armed with an edged weapon thirty feet away presents a deadly threat. This is because an average suspect can close that distance in less than two seconds, while the officer will take nearly that amount of time to recognize the danger, formulate a response, initiate the response mechanism, draw and point his weapon while moving to get off-line to the attack, and then pull the trigger. Then assuming everything works in the officer's favor—he accurately fires, hits the suspect, the bullet strikes and immediately impairs the brain-nerve function—the edged weapon may still strike and cut the officer due to the suspect's momentum.

Even if the officer fires two shots and gets good, center mass hits to the heart with both of them, the suspect will still have enough oxygenated blood and adrenaline in his system to keep attacking for another fifteen to twenty-five seconds. The officer can increase his odds by shooting on the move and moving laterally, but this assumes that these skill sets have been taught (which is a faulty assumption for the military in light of the ineffectiveness of most military firearms qualification courses) and practiced under high-stress conditions. Fifteen to twenty-five seconds of a still-armed assailant cutting, stabbing, and slashing—all the while the officer is left to defend himself close in with a handgun. The officer can continue shooting and hope that the suspect bleeds out more quickly or a round hits an area that will immediately disable the brain-nerve function, but the situation will be dangerous, violent, and bloody.

Our soldiers must be trained to recognize the fact that an insurgent, or an angry Haitian, with a machete (or baseball bat or paving stone) as distant as thirty feet or more may present an imminent threat of death or grievous bodily injury. This doesn't mean that they must shoot all those who pose threats of grievous bodily injury, rather that they may and it might be prudent to do so under the circumstances. Most importantly, however, any decision not to shoot such a subject should be a knowing and intelligent decision.

In the same knife-wielding situation described above, if one were to place a twelve-foot chain-link fence between the assailant and the officer, the opportunity for a subject to cause imminent harm to the officer would vanish. Much about an opportunity is situational, and the threat triangle is constantly moving and morphing, not subject to written rules or restrictions. That is why soldiers placed in situations where they must make deadly force decisions must be trained on threat recognition and judgment and not hampered with legally overly restrictive and confusing rules and matrices concerning the use of force.

Too often, critics of the JET seminar (mostly individuals who have neither been through the entire course nor deployed in combat) imply that law enforcement training is irrelevant to military missions or, worse, that JET teaches soldiers to be trigger-happy. Such critiques are misplaced, primarily because the SROE mandates that commanders at all levels instruct their subordinates on appropriate threat recognition and self-defense response, and the realities of law enforcement belie such concerns. In any given year over the past decade an average of 66,000 law enforcement officers have been assaulted. Of those assaults, over 16,500 were with a dangerous and deadly weapon, where, as a matter of law, deadly force would be authorized. Yet law enforcement only shot 800 subjects into the ground during that same time period. Hardly trigger-happy statistics.

It is imperative that such training be given not only to our warriors at the tip of the spear but also to the commanders and judge advocates that write the ROE and judge the uses of force after the fact. Without such knowledge, these people won't know what they don't know, and they will make judgments through a political lens rather than through a tactical lens. Military operations, by the design of our political structure, are necessarily political in nature. Warriors are often sent into dangerous and precarious situations in furtherance of our national interests. What should not happen, however, is for the political strategic objectives to dictate tactics in the life or death struggle at the tip of the spear.

The JET seminar is not a lone wolf in its efforts to transform military training from a rules-based to a judgment-based methodology. Author and retired military officer Donald Vandergriff cogently points out in the following passage some of the problems with current training, as well as some innovative solutions:

> As a result, recent leader and soldier training do not encourage thinking and decision making. In fact, it often discourages it. Although the best instructors—and especially those recently returned from combat—take great efforts to explain to their soldiers why things were done a certain way, the program itself stressed only the mechanical application of tasks. Worse, the atmosphere established during some courses emphasized "total control." In some units, particularly basic training units extended beyond the point of usefulness, that atmosphere sometimes remained nearly until graduation. Drill sergeants yelled, while instructors at leader courses assumed the "know and be all" stance that prevented anyone from questioning their authority. Cadets, candidates, and junior officers, as well as soldiers, asked few questions, and infractions were answered by mass punishment, while education techniques are rote and boring. The process for training mobilized Guardsmen and Reservists was even more obsolete and narrow.[136]

Vandergriff goes on to note that "young leaders and soldiers are not forced to work things out for themselves or to learn to be individually responsible. Not understanding why tasks are performed a certain way, they often fail to adapt properly to changed circumstances. Fortunately, thousands of leaders at the officer, NCO, and retired levels in the Army have recognized the downfalls of today's training and education doctrine and are moving from the bottom up to fix it, better preparing tomorrow's Army for the changing face of war."[137] Perhaps no other organization in the military embodies this more than the Army's Asymmetric Warfare Group (AWG).[138] AWG teaches the Combat Applications Training Course (CATC) using outcome-based training and education, which is a method to instruct and develop mastery of any given subject. Its premise is that soldiers can apply principles to understand the how and why of training. It takes the latest lessons learned in theaters of operations (war) and helps commanders and staffs translate these lessons into tactics, techniques, and procedures (TTPs). At the center of CATC, trainers use problem solving in order to teach a task. This is in contrast to the task-oriented training found in typical military training regimens. Task-oriented training works well, teaching skills with set procedures and static end states such as starting an aircraft or conducting pre-jump inspection of a paratrooper. This type of "check the block" training, while perhaps comforting to metrics-centric thinkers, does little to prepare individuals to make decisions in dynamic, tense situations like firefights.

To ignore the use of force training mandated in the SROE—"Unit Commanders at all levels shall ensure that individuals within their respective units understand and are trained on when and how to use force in self-defense"—is dangerous. To substitute overly restrictive ROE and ill-focused investigations in lieu of this mandate constitutes a systemic dereliction of duty. We owe it to our warriors to train them to the right legal and tactical standards. In doing so, we will better help them win and survive in today's deadly force encounters. Moreover, it will help America's strategic corporals reach the goals as outlined in current strategic doctrine.

Of course, the politically correct naysayers have already begun their passive-aggressive fight against such training because it challenges the status quo of the past twenty years—like the command to use minimum force and follow ROE cards. Instead of debating in an open academic forum, those that oppose adopting modern and realistic training make either ad hominem attacks against the messengers or make unsupportable claims, one of which is that these tactics teach soldiers to be trigger happy. The facts show that properly trained troops empowered to exercise their inherent right of self-defense will be much more likely to shoot people that need to be shot and much less likely to be attacked or to shoot noncombatants.

Another reason for some of the push-back from meddlers in the military—including many non-operationally savvy judge advocates—is that the idea that an individual soldier should have the authority and responsibility to actually kill someone flies in the face of their ivory-tower notions of precision, sterile warfare where only combatants get killed. In this regard, they mistake foolhardiness for chivalry.

Build a Warrior Ethos and Keep Soft Power out of the Military

Too many military theorists, strategists, and policy makers rely too much on the concept of soft power, as explained by one of its preeminent proponents, Joseph Nye:

> Everyone is familiar with hard power. We know that military and economic power might often get others to change their position. Hard power can rest on inducements ("carrots") or threats ("sticks"). But sometimes you can get the outcomes you want without tangible threats or payoffs. The indirect way to get what you want has sometimes been called "the second face of power." A country may obtain the outcomes it wants in world politics because other countries admire its values, emulate its example, aspire to its level of prosperity and openness. This soft power— getting others to want the outcomes that you want—co-opts people rather than coerces them.
>
> Soft power rests on the ability to shape the preferences of others. In the business world, smart executives know that leadership is not just a matter of issuing commands, but also involves leading by example and attracting others to do what you want. Similarly, contemporary practices of community-based policing rely on making the police sufficiently friendly and attractive that a community wants to help them achieve shared objectives.[139]

This is not to denigrate the efficacy and need for soft power. Rather it is an observation that many wish to transform the military from a coercive instrument to a soft-power instrument. Secretary of Defense Robert Gates spoke of the need to enhance American soft power by "a dramatic increase in spending on the civilian instruments of national security—diplomacy, strategic communications, foreign assistance, civic action and economic reconstruction and development."[140] Secretary Gates is spot on but needs to vigilantly stand guard against those seeking to use the military to take the lead in the application of soft power.

In fact, the best way the military can support other government agencies' soft-power efforts is to retain its martial virtues and skills. A strong and respected military can be a source of admiration for other nations. Friendly nations and potential allies will more readily seek military-to-military (mil-to-mil) cooperation and training programs offered by the United States if we remain strong. But our military will remain strong only if it retains the primary enduring martial virtues extolled throughout history. In light of many developments of the last two decades—even in time of war—this remains doubtful. If we continue down this road, we may face the same fate met by the fabled legions of the Roman Empire.

Commenting on the decline of the Roman Empire from a military perspective, historian Arther Ferrill quotes Flavius Vegetius Renatus:

> Footsoldiers wore breastplates and helmets. But when, because of negligence and laziness, parade ground drills were abandoned, the customary armour began to seem heavy since the soldiers rarely ever wore it. Therefore, they first asked the emperor to set aside the breastplates and mail and then the helmets. So our soldiers fought the Goths without any protection for chest and head and were often beaten by archers. Although there were many disasters, which led to the loss of the great cities, no one tried to restore breastplates and helmets to the infantry. Thus it happens that troops in battle, exposed to wounds because they have no armour, think about running and not about fighting.[141]

Similarly our modern military has become more concerned with mandatory equal opportunity and safety briefings, thumb-drive awareness, and myriad other issues decidedly not related to its ability to kill the enemy. Much of this is cultural. We have witnessed the softening of the military in many forms. Soldiers are prohibited from singing martial and lusty cadences for fear that they may offend. Marine Force Reconnaissance (Force Recon) units have proscribed the ritual of blood wings (the good-natured pounding of the coveted gold navy parachutist wings into the chest of newly-minted marine paratroopers after their eleventh jump). And God forbid if an American warrior returns from combat with weapons, flags, or other war booty or trophies. The tsk-tsking from the combined judge advocate and flag officer circles will quickly be followed up by inordinately long and painful investigations. To what end? Do we think that our vanquished enemies will respect us more because we do not let our soldiers take home a bayonet?

This trend in the military is especially absurd because the warrior elements of our military have never pretended to be a part of society at large in their lifestyle, their methods of training, or mission parameters. Soldiers' and marines' sense of loyalty, esprit de corps, and pride in their ability to fight is not something transmutable to or compatible with genteel concepts of social reform. An average person may be offended because he or she is "subjected to a hostile work environment," but an average warrior's response is "Suck it up!" This response is the correct response. As to the individual, if one is not thick-skinned enough to rebuff a perceived social affront, how can he be expected to withstand the rigors of combat or the training it takes to withstand such rigors? While the military's demographic structure should ideally mirror the general populace, it should never sacrifice its core principles and focus in an attempt to do so. This is not to say that soldiers can't be gentlemen and women, but rather that we should not be more concerned with indoctrinating them into the latest politically correct fad (witness the latest craze of forcing soldiers to endure day after day of briefings on accepting gays in the military). We should focus instead on providing hard, realistic training on how to kill the enemy. One may argue that political correctness and a warrior ethos are not mutually exclusive. Individually, this may be true. It is the systemic Orwellian mass reeducation, however, which reflects a dangerous shift in the soul of our military. This radical shift is destroying our future ability to fight and win a major conflict.

These trends in policy have created a schizophrenic military leadership often more concerned with stamping out profanity and sexual harassment than with winning wars. And can you blame them when warriors like Mike Steele are given career-ending head shots for inculcating a warrior mentality amongst their troops in combat? Political correctness has degraded morale and will ultimately lead to a military society with the ethos of social workers rather than warriors.

Political forces may see it as desirable to advocate for yet more social change in the military. Most likely, their ignorance is based on the fact that less than a quarter of the current crop in Congress has served in the military. Unfortunately, many young Americans will get killed in battle before those in Congress realize the value of maintaining a solid cadre of steely-eyed killers rather than politically correct peacemakers.

Part of the problem is the fact that most senior military leaders have had no real experience with close-quarters combat and are not truly proficient with their small arms. This may sound surprising to the American public, but these leaders simply don't know what they don't know. While skilled in some of the arts of war—maneuver, command and control, and the use of high-tech intelligence, surveillance, and reconnaissance (ISR) assets—they are woefully ignorant of the dynamics of close and personal violence. They don't know that minimum force is a tactically inappropriate response to an imminent threat of death or serious bodily injury. They don't know that the realities of action-reaction do not allow one to "wait until the enemy points his weapon at you before engaging" or that a fleeing hostile actor presents a continuing threat to oneself and innocent others. They only know that the COIN doctrine abhors civilian casualties.

And the solution is not simply to call all soldiers, sailors, airmen, or marines "warriors" or give out more badges and berets. Rather, from basic military training onward, tough martial virtues should be inculcated and rewarded. Ground fighting, enduring weapons-intimacy skills training, and rigorous combined-arms training should be requirements, not the exception, for all leaders as well as their subordinate forces.

Building Stronger Bonds within the Force

Just as it was when we fought the ideological war against the communist threat for the forty years after World War II, a fundamental belief in the supremacy of the American way of life is a necessary component for success. While there will always be diverse thought and beliefs in a free society, it is not productive to unnecessarily encourage rancor and discord among ourselves. America, specifically her military, needs to move away from the trend of hyphenating our culture: African-American, Hispanic-American, Native-American, and so on. We are American soldiers, sailors, airmen, and marines, period. Instead of trumpeting the positive aspects that cultural diversity brings to a groups' critical and creative thinking abilities, the military's efforts at diversity training and cultural awareness do nothing but highlight skin-deep differences instead of reinforcing stronger bonds.

We have created a cult of diversity that encourages individuals to see themselves as aligned with groups rather than with a unified American effort. The military has even created the Defense Equal Opportunity Management Institute (DEOMI) at Patrick Air Force Base in Florida just to address this issue. This diversity training betrays a solemn oath to forge a unified fighting force irrespective of color or creed. The soldiers, sailors, airmen, and marines at the tip of the spear recognize this. They are more interested in receiving top-of-the-line equipment, more ammunition, and realistic tactical training than mandatory EO training.

The military constantly "celebrates diversity." Unfortunately, this has had a corrosive and segregating effect on the force. We have created a cult of diversity that encourages individuals to see themselves as aligned with a racial group rather than with a unified American effort. While not a problem in combat at the moment—the threat and peril of death generally has a wonderfully annealing effect—it will continue to erode the fiber and unified direction of the force unless corrected.

For an individual in uniform to even question the cult of diversity will invite a reign of terror from on high. Officer evaluation reports (OERs) in the army even have a special block that reflects that the rated officer supports EO/EEO.[142]

Rather than enforcing a degree of excellence and conformity, the race baiters and diversity police have set up a false dichotomy that threatens excellence and achievement. The military has swallowed this "celebration of diversity" hook, line, and sinker. Celebration of diversity should only come about by the recognition of individual achievement and excellence. If a soldier is a great leader, he should be celebrated as such. Not as a great "Scots-American" leader or "Hispanic-American" leader, but a great American leader. Why celebrate and foment diversity when we are supposed to be a unified force? We should be celebrating warriors.

This worshipping at the altar of diversity needs to be replaced in the military by an overt and proud "Army of Green" or "Air Force Blue" esprit de corps that focuses solely on developing a warrior class regardless of color or creed. Commanders should focus on inclusion and unity, not diversity. Spending countless hours focusing on differences, the military completely misses the mark of truly effective leadership: focusing a diverse group into a unified, spirited warrior class. The Spartans were not a highly effective warrior class because of their diversity. Rather, they were all Spartans. Similarly, the military should be drilling the fact that we are all Americans into the culture and mores of its ranks. An American warrior class will result that is much more resilient and effective at killing our enemies.

We should heed the advice of G. K. Chesterton who said, "The voice of the special rebels and prophets, recommending discontent, should, as I have said, sound now and then suddenly, like a trumpet. But the voices of the saints and sages, recommending contentment, should sound unceasingly, like the sea."[143] The future prosperity and security of the peoples of Western Civilization depends on the unified, strengthened resolve of its people. None more so than its warrior class. We are involved in a cultural and kinetic struggle with a determined enemy. Developing, training, and preparing the military to perform warlike tasks to face current and future threats will preserve its strength as well as our peace.

How the military should deal with Muslims within its ranks is not even being asked or addressed by true critical thinking methodologies within the military hierarchy. This is not an attack on freedom of religion, but rather a simple question of how to deal with individuals who choose to place their allegiance to Allah over their duties as citizens and Soldiers of the United States. If one's personal religious beliefs are incompatible with service—service that may include killing fellow Muslims—then that individual should not be allowed into the military. If, after accession, an individual voices opinions that are incompatible with military service, then the military has a duty to remove such a threat from its ranks.

The Explosion of the Military Industrial Complex

The honor code at the U.S. Military Academy states, "A cadet will not lie, cheat, steal, or tolerate those who do." This may be enough for an officer to successfully navigate at command levels all the way to brigade command, but more is needed at the strategic leadership level.

Some may argue that if by the twenty-year service level an officer does not have his basic moral compass in order, then there is no amount of education or training that can correct such a deficiency. Even if true, this assertion misses the point. First, the services should identify and remove people who have made it through two decades of service with a flawed understanding of ethics in professional life.

Instruction on leadership necessarily requires teaching virtues. Alexandre Harvard, in his book, *Virtuous Leadership: An Agenda for Personal Excellence*, echoes these sentiments: "Virtues . . . are part and parcel of [professional competence] and substantially so." Professional competence implies the application of technical knowledge to some "fruitful purpose."[144]

Our country requires senior officers who can apply an innate sense of virtue so that their decisions reflect well on their profession and inspire trust and confidence in their countrymen. UNC Chapel Hills' Richard H. Kohn, no stranger to the military, is equally direct:

> Related to these strategic and political failures are possible moral deficiencies among the officer corps, which have arisen in the last few years. At its heart is a growing careerism that has led to micromanagement from above and a sense that any defect will derail a career, which in turn leads to risk aversion and sometimes to cover-ups, avoidance of responsibility, and other behaviors that harm the ability of the armed forces to succeed in battle.[145]

Kohn, however, ranks moral deficiencies third behind a lack of intellectual rigor and political savvy. While his arguments are sound, the lack of moral structure and virtuous leadership may be the preeminent factor driving the other two problems.

Either out of hubris or woeful ignorance, most in Washington—and, unfortunately, the Pentagon—are simply incapable of recognizing simplicity of manners and a zeal for honor. In the end, all Americans can do is pray and vote. However, one must remain heedful of the following truths as cogently pointed out by 5th Special Forces, Republic of Vietnam veteran Sean Fitzpatrick:

Our liberty is from God not the government;

Our sovereignty is in our souls not the soil;

Our security is from strength not surrender;

Our prosperity is from the private sector not the public sector; and,

Our truths are self-evident not relative.

The military is not totally blameless in the exponential growth of the federal government. With military budgets that absorb approximately 50 percent of the nation's discretionary spending, when was the last time a commander was rewarded for saying "We need less" or "Do we really need that multibillion dollar weapon system?" Leaders at all levels go into fourth-quarter-of-the-fiscal year spending sprees so they don't have a surplus at the end of the year because if their commands have a surplus, or do not spend all they are given in the fiscal year, then their budgets are cut the next year. Yet no one questions this lack of integrity, or perhaps lying to, stealing from, and cheating the taxpayers just doesn't count. This race to spend must stop.

Unlike private corporations where leaders are responsible to the shareholders or owners, the Pentagon's service chiefs make fiscal decisions not in the interest of the greater enterprise, but rather in the interests of their individual services. The Joint Requirements Oversight Council (JROC) is a congressionally mandated internal system that is supposed to review and validate all Acquisition Category I and IA (big ticket) programs and other programs designated as high interest. The JROC is chaired by the Vice Chairman of the Joint Chiefs of Staff, who also serves as the co-chair of the Defense Acquisition Board. The other JROC members are the vice chiefs of each military service. But at JROC meetings, no four-star member will undercut another service's pet program for fear of reciprocal cuts to their own pet projects. The defense contractors and project managers, as well as the generals and admirals in charge, continue in this manner because that is the world they know. The integrity of the system is flawed because there are no incentives for doing what is right. For the past five decades the service budgets have remained roughly evenly divided: a third navy, a third army, and a third air force. It is a quid pro quo system that no one dares to question, especially those within the system who rely on its progenitors for ratings and promotion.

We need a strong hand at the helm of the Department of Defense to abolish policies that promote mission creep and profligate and service-selfish spending. That strong hand will receive intense resistance from the generals and Congress alike, but such leadership is necessary to help cauterize the runaway budgets. We need strong leaders to refocus the military to resume its more traditional missions of killing or destroying our enemies and keeping us safe.

The immediate future, however, does not look bright. Civilian policy makers too quickly turn to the military to solve their diplomatic problems. In a March 3, 2010, speech at Kansas State University, Chairman of the Joint Chiefs of Staff, Admiral Mike Mullen, stated:

> It's one thing to be able and willing to serve as emergency responders; quite another to always have to be the fire chief.
>
> Secretaries Clinton and Gates have called for more funding and more emphasis on our soft power, and I could not agree with them more. Should we choose to exert American influence solely through our troops, we should expect to see that influence diminish in time. In fact, I would argue that in the future struggles of the asymmetric counterinsurgent variety, we ought to make it a precondition of committing our troops, that we will do so only if and when the other instruments of national power are ready to engage as well.[146]

Policy makers and some military strategists' worship at the COIN/VUCA altar will increase both defense spending and mission creep. More frighteningly, it will seriously blunt America's ability to conduct force-on-force combat with near-peer competitors or other unforeseen threats that may arise due to the ubiquity of information and technology. The Department of Defense budget already chews up 50 percent of the United States' discretionary budget: a budget that is unsustainable in these days of $17 trillion deficits. It is only prudent that the dollars spent should be focused on warfighting and defensive capabilities rather than never-ending efforts at nation-building and peacekeeping operations.

CONCLUSION

In raising the issues we've discussed, the authors realize that some readers might take offense. We hope this book will start a dialogue and discussion in the public forum with a view toward reaching rigorously reasoned solutions to the problems presented. These problems will not go away simply because we ignore them. In fact, they will only fester with age.

American exceptionalism, nationalism, and patriotism are not dirty or shameful words. Any intellectuals or bourgeoisiephobes out there who think otherwise should be called out as enemies of the republic when they presume to give their quisling advice to our strategic leaders. You can't serve two masters, yet that is exactly what these people are doing when they encourage America to surrender fundamental values and her sovereignty to an international supernumerary. Anyone who is embarrassed by expressing the belief that our constitutional republic has been the best experiment on the governance of man should be shunned.

Too often we delude ourselves into believing that if we demonstrate our tolerance by surrendering critical elements of our social norms, then other cultures will like and respect us. History has shown the opposite to be true time and again. True patriots must keep their "hatchets scoured and powder dry," as Rogers' Rangers said during the French-Indian War. There may come a day when either the internationalists or the Islamists will come knocking on American doors.

To the warriors at the tip of the spear: Keep your moral compass pointed in the right direction and never surrender your right of individual or unit self-defense. The strategic missions may be misguided, but your individual sacrifices are the stuff of legend. Come home whole, both physically and spiritually, and be there to tell your kids and grandkids what you did in America's wars.

The United States military faces multiple threats in the near and distant future, threats from enemies—state and stateless—who are unafraid of waging unrestricted warfare on our way of life.[147] While we should never surrender our adherence to a rule of law centered on our constitutional principles and the ethical conduct of war, we must restore reason and logic to how such rules are applied to our forces in combat. If we lose the republic by our failure to do so, the rules will be rewritten by our enemies. One should have little reason to believe that the Islamists or communist Chinese, if victorious, will afford much respect to the freedoms we enjoy and cherish.

As a nation, the public and the policy makers should demand martial excellence and superiority of the military force, which should only be used to affect a military purpose. Our foes will better understand and respect us and be less likely to attack. Predators don't generally prey on those who look like they are hunting. If we continue down the road of turning our military into purveyors of diplomacy and masters of stability operations, our future generations will be speaking Arabic or Mandarin Chinese.

NOTES

1. Michael T. Flynn, Matt Pottinger, Paul D. Batchelor, *Fixing Intel: A Blueprint for Making Intelligence Relevant in Afghanistan*, Center for a New American Security (CNAS), January 2010.
2. http://www.pbs.org/wgbh/pages/frontline/shows/military/etc/estes.html
3. Colonel Thomas Sheperd, Department of National Security and Strategy, U.S. Army War College, Carlisle, Pennsylvania, in a discussion with David G. Bolgiano, February 8, 2010, used with permission.
4. Liz Goodwin, "How Much Will Our Wars Cost?" The Lookout, A YNews Blog, June 29, 2011. http://news.yahoo.com/blogs/lookout/much-wars-cost-report-says-4-trillion-130934180.html
5. Winston S. Churchill, *Memoirs of the Second World War: An Abridgement of the Six Volumes of The Second World War*, Houghton Mifflin, Boston, 1959, p. 855.
6. Gilles Dorronsoro, *Fixing a Failed Strategy in Afghanistan*, Carnegie Endowment for International Peace, Washington, D.C., 2009.
7. Montgomery McFate, Ph.D., and Andrea V. Jackson, "The Object Beyond War: Counter-Insurgency and the Four Tools of Political Competition," *Military Review*, January/February 2006, p. 14.
8. This thought was originally raised to the authors by Jeff Spears of L-3Com during a conversation on national security; unfortunately, many senior leaders lack Jeff's prescience.
9. Christopher D. Kolenda, "Winning Afghanistan at the Community Level: A Rejoinder to Volney F. Warner and 'C'," *Joint Force Quarterly*, NDU Press, January 2010.
10. CJCS Guidance for 2009–2010, December 21, 2009, p. 6.
11. Michael J. Mazarr, "The Folly of 'Asymmetric War'," *The Washington Quarterly*, Summer 2008, p. 33.

12. Daniel G. Cox, "The Struggle Against Global Insurgency," *Joint Force Quarterly*, NDU Press, January 2010.

13. Michael Scheuer, *Marching Toward Hell: America and Islam after Iraq*, Free Press, New York, 2008, p. 71.

14. Michael V. Hayden, "Obama Administration Takes Several Wrong Paths in Dealing with Terrorism," *The Washington Post*, January 31, 2010.

15. Stephen L. Coughlin, "'To Our Great Detriment:' Ignoring What Extremists Say About Jihad," Unclassified thesis submitted in support of Masters of Science in Strategic Intelligence Degree, National Defense Intelligence College, July 2007.

16. Coughlin, Ibid., quoting Steven Kull, *Muslim Public Opinion on US Policy, Attacks on Civilians and al Qaeda*, WorldPublicOpinion.org (Program on International Policy Attitudes, University of Maryland, Washington, D.C., April 24, 2007).

17. Sun Tzu, *The Art of War*, Chapter 1, Strategic Assessments.

18. Osama bin Laden, "Jihad Against Jews and Crusaders," February 23, 1998.

19. See e.g., Mark Steyn, *America Alone: The End of the World as We Know It*, Regnery Publishing, Washington, D.C., 2006.

20. Charles Krauthammer, "Medicalizing Mass Murder," *The Washington Post*, November 13, 2009.

21. Togo West and Vern Clark, *Protecting the Force: Lessons from Fort Hood*, Report of the Independent Review, Department of Defense, January 2010.

22. Ibid., p. 32.

23. Anne Gearan, "Pentagon to Adopt Uniform Rules on Guns," The Associated Press, April 16, 2010.

24. Levi Pulkkinen and Scott Gutierrez, "Seattle Man Implicated in Plot to Blow Up Military Recruiting Station," *SeattlePI*, June 23, 2001, http://www.seattlepi.com/local/article/Seattle-man-implicated-in-plot-to-blow-up-1437405.php#ixzz1QDPzo7Ea.

25. Charles J. Dunlap Jr., "Lawfare Today," *Yale Journal of International Affairs*, Winter 2008, p. 146. Major General Dunlap, while not inventing the term "lawfare," is certainly the author most cited and credited with expounding on its meaning and relevance in the making of modern strategy.

26. Samuel Helfont, "Islam and Islamism Today: The Case of Yusuf Al-Qaradawi," Foreign Policy Research Institute E-note, January 12, 2010, based on Helfont's book, *Yusuf al-Qaradawi: Islam and Modernity*, Moshe Dayan Center, Tel Aviv University, 2009.

27. Ruth Gledhill and Richard Owen, "Carey Backs Pope and Issues Warning on 'Violent' Islam," *The London Times*, September 20, 2006.

28. Henry Kissinger, "Obama Is Like a Chess Player," *Spiegel Online*, July 6, 2009.

29. Andrew Gregorovich, "The Cossack Letter," Forum, A Ukrainian Review Page, http://www.infoukes.com/history/cossack_letter/.

30. Ray Takeyh and Nikolas K. Gvosdev, "Radical Islam: The Death of an Ideology?" *Middle East Policy*, Vol. XI, No. 4, Winter 2004.

31. Hugo Grotius, *The Law of War and Peace*, Chap. 22, V, 1.

32. Associated Press, "Taliban Fighters Step Up Attacks on U.S., Afghan Troops in Marjah," February 15, 2010.

33. "Interpretive Guidance on the Notion of Direct Participation in Hostilities Under International Humanitarian Law," International Committee of the Red Cross, Geneva, May 2009, p. 68.

34. John Yoo, *War by Other Means*, Atlantic Monthly Press, 2006, p.36.

35. Sun Tzu, *The Art of War*, Translated by Samuel B. Griffith, Oxford University Press, London, 1963, p. 77.

36. Samantha Newberry, Bob Brecher, Philippe Sands, "Interrogation, Intelligence and the Issue of Human Rights," *Intelligence and National Security*, Vol. 24, No. 5, October 2009, p. 643.

37. Evan Wallach, "Waterboarding Used to Be a Crime," *The Washington Post*, November 4, 2007.

38. E.g., The Rule of Law and the Global War on Terrorism Symposium, held November 13 and 14, 2008, at the Bradbury Thompson Alumni Center on the Washburn University campus. The symposium was hosted by the Washburn University School of Law Center for Law and Government and the *Washburn Law Journal*.

39. Mackubin Thomas Owens, "The Pirates Challenge Obama's Pre-9/11 Mentality: Distinctions Between Lawful and Unlawful Combatants Go Back to Roman Times," *The Wall Street Journal*, April 11, 2009.

40. Clint Wood, "Striking Fear from Far Away: Becoming a Sniper," *GX Magazine*, Vol. 7, Issue 2, March/April 2010, p. 49.

41. Barrett Tillman, "Let's Arm the Force," *Proceedings*, Naval Institute, January 2010, p. 10.

42. Ibid.

43. Franklin C. Spinney, "Pork Barrels and Budgeteers: What Went Wrong with the Quadrennial Defense Reviews?" *Strategic Review*, Fall 1997, p. 29.

44. David G. Bolgiano, *Combat Self-Defense: Saving America's Warriors from Risk-averse Commanders and Their Lawyers*, Little White Wolf Books, Severna Park, 2007.

45. Michael Sheuer, *Marching Toward Hell: America and Islam after Iraq*, Free Press, New York, 2008, pp. 81–82.

46. From Holmes speech, "The Soldier's Faith," delivered on Memorial Day, May 30, 1895, to the graduating class of Harvard University.

47. *Brown v. United States*, 256 U.S. 335, 343 (1921).

48. Robert G. Delaney, "Army Transformation: The Human Condition of Soldiering," *Military Review*, May–June 2004, p. 37, citing U.S. Army Regimental Training Circular 350-1-2, Close Quarters Combat Program of Instruction.

49. Major General Eldon Bargewell, USA (Ret.), in an interview with the author, August 2007. General Bargewell began his 40-year Army career as a Special Forces Soldier in Vietnam, where he was awarded, among other awards and decorations, the Distinguished Service Cross. Throughout his

career, he served at various levels of command, including command of 1st Special Forces Operational Detachment—Delta (Delta Force). He has also been awarded the Purple Heart on four occasions.

50. To gain a glimpse into the intensity of the fighting endured during the building of the wall around Sadr City, see "Battle of Sadr City," which first aired on CBS News' *60 Minutes*, October 12, 2008, http://www.cbsnews. com/stories/2008/10/09/60minutes/main4511800.shtml   or   http://www. youtube.com/watch?v=qGpqXDbkp-M.

51. Memorandum Opinion (J. Urbina), *United States v. Paul A. Slough et al*, Criminal Action No.: 08-0360 (RMU), United States District Court for the District of Columbia, December 31, 2009, p. 22.

52. Memorandum Opinion (J. Urbina), Ibid., p. 23.

53. BBC, "Biden Vows the US Will Appeal in Iraq Blackwater Case," January 23, 2010.

54. Greg Jaffe, "U.S. Commanders in Afghanistan Face Tougher Discipline for Battlefield Failures," *The Washington Post*, February 5, 2010.

55. Barbara Starr, "U.S. and NATO Troops in Afghanistan Could Someday Be Awarded Medals for Restraint that Prevents Civilian Casualties in Combat," CNN U.S., May 12, 2010.

56. Winston S. Churchill, *Memoirs of the Second World War: An Abridgement of the Six Volumes of The Second World War*, Houghton Mifflin, Boston, 1959, Note 4, p. 495.

57. Sun Tzu, *The Art of War*, Translated by Samuel B. Griffith, Oxford University Press, London, 1963.

58. Alexander Schwabe, "The Cowboy and the Shepherd," *Spiegel Online International*, April 16, 2008.

59. http://en.wikiquote.org/wiki/Winston_Churchill, unsourced.

60. Thomas E. Ricks, "COIN Commander Reveals: Here's What Worked for Me in Ramadi," *Foreign Policy*, February 3, 2010, quoting an unpublished paper by Sean McFarland.

61. Thomas W. McShane, "International Law and the New World Order: Redefining Sovereignty," reprinted in *U.S. Army War College Guide to National Security Issues, Vol. 2: National Security Policy and Strategy*, Edited by J. Boone Bartholomees Jr., Carlisle barracks, Pennsylvania, June 2008.

62. Winston Churchill, *The Grand Alliance*, Edited by John Keegan, Houghton Mifflin Books, New York, 1986.

63. Letter from Daniel Webster, Secretary of State, to Henry Fox, British Minister in Washington, April 24, 1841, reprinted in John Bassett Moore, *A Digest of International Law*, 409, 412 (GPO, 1906).

64. Lieutenant Commander Dale Stephens, "Rules of Engagement and the Concept of Unit Self Defense," 45 *NAVAL LAW REVIEW*, 126, 134 (1998).

65. Hans Kelsen, *Collective Security Under International Law*, Naval War College, Newport, Rhode Island, 2001.

66. See "International Military Tribunal (Nuremberg), Judgment and Sentences," reprinted in 41 *American Journal of International Law* 172, 205 (1947): "Preventive action in foreign territory is justified only in case of 'an instant and overwhelming necessity for self-defense, leaving no choice of means, and no moment for deliberation,'", quoting John Bassett Moore, *A Digest of International Law*, § 217 at 412 (GPO, 1906).

67. Winston Churchill, *The Grand Alliance*, Edited by John Keegan, Houghton Mifflin Books, New York, 1986, Note 3.

68. Mark Matthews, "President's One-Year Troop Commitment to Bosnia Is Called Unrealistic, Political," *The Baltimore Sun*, December 2, 1995.

69. Nened Sebak, "The KLA—Terrorists or Freedom Fighters," *BBC Online*, June 28, 1998.

70. John Harlow, "Army Unveils New Stability Operations Manual," Army Website, October 6, 2008, http://www.army.mil/article/13079/army-unveils-new-stability-operations-manual/.

71. http://afghanistan.hmg.gov.uk/en/conference/communique/

72. Quoted in Executive Summary, *Joint Force Quarterly*, Issue 56, 1st Quarter 2010, p. 16, citing Jim Gant, *One Tribe at a Time*, Nine Sisters Imports, Los Angeles, 2009, p. 8.

73. Paul Yingling, "A Failure in Generalship," *Armed Forces Journal*, May 2007.

74. Raffi Khatchadourian, "The Kill Company: Did a Colonel's Fiery Rhetoric Set the Conditions for a Massacre?" *The New Yorker*, July 6, 2009.

75. John Ramsey, "Fort Bragg Battalion Commander Relieved of Duty in Afghanistan," *Fayetteville Observer*, January 23, 2010.

76. Oracle Homeland Security Solutions, "Leveraging Information Technology to Secure America," 2003, quoting Winston Churchill, http://www.oracle.com/industries/ government/ Oracle_in_Homeland_Security.pdf.

77. Charles C. Krulak, "The Strategic Corporal: Leadership in the Three Block War," *Marines Magazine*, January 1999.

78. Marcus Tullius Cicero, *Defense Speeches, On Behalf of Milo, 60 BCE*, Translated by D. H. Berry, Oxford University Press, London, 2000.

79. William Blackstone, *Commentaries on the Laws of England*, 1766, 3, at 141.

80. Ibid.

81. John Locke, *Two Treatises of Government*, "The State of War," 1689, §16.

82. Ibid.

83. William Hawkins, *Pleas of the Crown*, 7th ed., 1795, 1, Chapter 28, §14.

84. William Blackstone, *Commentaries on the Laws of England*, 1766, at 141.

85. Constitution Society, "Samuel Adams, The Rights of Colonists, November 20, 1772," http://www.constitution.org/bcp/right_col.htm.

86. David Blair, "UN Commander Says Hands Are Tied in Congo," *The Daily Telegraph*, London, November 17, 2008.

87. CJCSI 3121.01B, June 13, 2005.

88. Paul K. Van Riper, "EBO There Was No Baby in the Bathwater," *Joint Force Quarterly*, Issue 52, 1st Quarter 2009.

89. CJCSI 3121.01B June 13, 2005.

90. Undisclosed noncommissioned officer (NCO) e-mail to the author, October 12, 2007. The NCO's duties included providing squad-level escort duties to civilian members of diverse inter-agency task forces in the Iraqi theater.

91. "Panel Clears Army Sniper of Murder Charges in Iraq," *Seattle Times*, November 9, 2007. "The court-martial panel cleared Staff Sgt. Michael Hensley of three counts of murder and also of charges that he made false statements to investigators. He was found guilty of placing an AK-47 assault rifle on a man killed May 11 by a fellow soldier. Hensley also was convicted on two counts of insubordination for walking away from and cursing an officer."

92. Colonel Ben Corell, USA, U.S. Army War College Class of 2009, Seminar 4, interview by author Bolgiano, October 15, 2008.

93. From the author's duties, observations, and readings concerning diverse classified and unclassified situation reports from both Iraq and Afghanistan from March 2007 until June 2008. At the time, the author was working as Deputy General Counsel, Joint IED Defeat Organization, Counter IED Operational Integration Center (JIEDDO-COIC).

94. E.g., Chicago Police Department General Order 02-08-03, Section III stating in pertinent part that "[an officer may use deadly force against an escaping subject if the officer reasonably believes]:
    a. has committed or has attempted to commit a forcible felony involving the infliction, threatened infliction, or threatened use of physical force likely to cause death or great bodily harm or;
    b. is attempting to escape by use of a deadly weapon or;
    c. otherwise indicates that he or she will endanger human life or inflict great bodily harm unless arrested without delay."

95. United States Army's Center for Law and Military Operations (CLAMO) e-mail message to deployed legal offices, January 16, 2008.

96. Major General Harrell made these comments in 2006 in a videotaped interview for the Navy's Center for Security Forces as it was developing its own Judgment-based Engagement Training for its Riverine Forces. General Harrell formerly commanded Special Operations Command Central during OEF and OIF, 1st Special Forces Operational Detachment-Delta (Delta Force), and at the company, troop, and squadron level commands at that unit.

97. *Graham v. Connor*, 490 U.S. 386 (1989).

98. Lieutenant Colonel Kyle Siegel, Connecticut Air National Guard, was the genius behind this fictional construct. The Sam Damon name is a literary reference to Anton Myers's military classic *Once an Eagle*.

99. Thomas W. McShane, "International Law and the New World Order: Redefining Sovereignty," *U.S. Army War College Guide to National Security Issues, Volume II: National Security Policy and Strategy*, Edited by J.

Boone Bartholomees Jr., Department of National Security and Strategy, June 2008, p. 221, quoting, Legality of the Threat or Use of Nuclear Weapons, International Court of Justice, July 8, 1996, Declaration of President Bedjaoui at para. 13., quoted in Robert F. Turner, "Nuclear Weapons and the World Court: The ICJ's Advisory Opinion and Its Significance for U.S. Strategic Doctrine," *U.S. Naval War College International Law Studies*, Vol. 72, Michael N. Schmitt, Newport, ed., Naval War College Press, Annapolis, 1998, pp. 309, 312.

100.   Kofi A. Annan, "Two Concepts of Sovereignty," *The Economist*, September 18, 1999, p. 49.

101.   Center for Strategic and International Studies' Global Strategic Institute, "Seven Revolutions," http://csis.org/program/seven-revolutions.

102.   Sarah Sewall, "The International Criminal Court," Carr Center for Human Rights Policy Working Paper T-00-02, Harvard Kennedy School, 2000, p. 7.

103.   David E. Graham, "A Long, Hard Fall from the Pedestal," *Joint Force Quarterly*, Issue 54, 3rd quarter 2009, p. 30.

104.   William F. Buckley Jr., *Gratitude: Reflections on What We Owe to Our Country*, Random House, New York, 1990, p. xxi.

105.   5 United States Code § 3331. See also Department of the Army (DA) Form 71, July 1999.

106.   Michael L. Smidt, "The International Criminal Court: An Effective Means of Deterrence?," *Military Law Review*, Vol. 167, 2001, p. 219, citing U.S. Constitution, art, III, § 1, and Cara Levy Rodriguez, "Slaying the Monster: Why the United States Should Not Support the Rome Treaty," 14 *American University International Law Review*, 805, at 815.

107.   U.S. Constitution Amendment IV. "The right of the people to be secure in their persons, houses, papers, and effects, against unreasonable searches and seizures, shall not be violated, and no Warrants shall issue, but upon probable cause, supported by Oath or affirmation, and particularly describing the place to be searched, and the persons or things to be seized."

108.   U.S. Constitution Amendment VI. "In all criminal prosecutions, the accused shall enjoy the right to a speedy and public trial, by an impartial jury of the State and district wherein the crime shall have been committed, which district shall have been previously ascertained by law, and to be informed of the nature and cause of the accusation; to be confronted with the witnesses against him; to have compulsory process for obtaining witnesses in his favor, and to have the Assistance of Counsel for his defence."

109.   David Stoelting, book review of *International Criminal Law and Human Rights*, by Claire de Than & Edwin Shorts (Sweet and Maxwell, London, 2003) 550 pages in *Human Rights Quarterly*, 27.4, 2005, pp. 1365–1367.

110.   Michael L. Smidt, "The International Criminal Court: An Effective Means of Deterrence?," *Military Law Review*, Vol. 167, 2001, p. 203, quoting Hearing on the Creation of an International Criminal Court Before the

Subcommittee on International Operations of the Committee on Foreign Relations, 105th Cong. 60, 1998, statement of Sen. Helms.

111. Smidt, Ibid., p. 203, citing Walter Gary Sharp Sr., "Revoking an Aggressor's License to Kill Military Forces Serving the United Nations: Making Deterrence Personal," 22 *Maryland Journal of International Law and Trade*, 1, 1998.

112. Smidt, Ibid., p. 212, citing Mark Husban, "Spectators Pay High Price in Somalia Theater," *London Times Observer*, September 12, 1993, p. 12.

113. The late Congressman Murtha stated, "There was no firefight. There was no IED that killed these innocent people. Our troops overreacted because of the pressure on them, and they killed innocent civilians in cold blood." *NBC Nightly News*, May 17, 2006. See Civil Complaint, *Wuterich v. Murtha*, United States District Court for the District of Columbia, p. 20.

114. John Midgley, "Warning: The European Union and Political Correctness," The Bruges Group, London, http://www.brugesgroup.com/mediacentre/comment.live?article=8963.

115. *The Queen v. Lee William Clegg*, In the Crown Court of Northern Ireland, November 3, 1999.

116. See U.N. Human Rights Council, Subcommission on the Promotion and Protection of Human Rights, 58th Session, Adoption of the Report on the Fifty-eighth Session to the Human Rights Council, U.N. Doc. A/HRC/Sub.1/58/L.11/Add.1, August 24, 2006, http://hrp.cla.umn.edu/documents/ A.HRC.Sub.1.58.L.11.Add.1.pdf.

117. David B. Kopel, Paul Galant, and Joanne D. Eisen, "The Human Right of Self-Defense," *BYU Journal of Public Law*, Vol. 22, Winter 2008.

118. Noah Feldman, "When Judges Make Foreign Policy," *New York Times (Sunday Magazine)*, September 28, 2008.

119. Erik Gorski, "Report: Global Muslim Population Hits 1.57 Billion," The Associated Press, October 8, 2009.

120. Alan M. Dershowitz, "The Hypocrisy of Universal Jurisdiction," *Hudson New York*, an online feature of Hudson Institute, October 6, 2009. Mr. Dershowitz is the Felix Frankfurter Professor of Law at Harvard Law School.

121. Stephen C. Coughlin, "To Our Great Detriment: Ignoring What Extremists Say About Jihad," Unclassified thesis submitted in support of Masters of Science in Strategic Intelligence Degree, National Defense Intelligence College, July 2007, p.10, quoting Sheikh 'Abdullah bin Muhammad bin Humaid, Chief Justice of Saudi Arabia, Appendix III: "The Call to Jihad (Holy Fighting for Allah in the Qur'an Statement)," located in *Interpretation of the Meanings of the Noble Qur'an in the English Language: A Summarized Version of At-Tabari; Al-Qurtubi, and Ibn Kathir with Comments from Sahih Al-Bukhari*, Translated and commentary by Dr. Muhammad Taqi-ud-Din Al-Hilali, and Dr. Muhammad Muhsin Khan, Darussalam, Riyadh, Saudi Arabia, 1995, pp. 963, 964.

122. The Organization of the Islamic Conference (OIC), http://www.oic-oci.org.

123. Cairo Declaration on Human Rights in Islam.

124. Ibid., Preamble.

125. Ibid.

126. Ibid., Article 24 and 25.

127. Stephen C. Coughlin, "To Our Great Detriment: Ignoring What Extremists Say About Jihad," Unclassified thesis submitted in support of Masters of Science in Strategic Intelligence Degree, National Defense Intelligence College, July 2007, p. 79.

128. Mary Habeck, "Teaching the Long War and Jihadism," an essay based on her presentation at U.S. Foreign Policy and the Modern Middle East, a Summer Institute for Teachers sponsored by The American Institute for History Education and The Wachman Center of the Foreign Policy Research Institute, June 25–27, 2009, in Philadelphia. Copyright Foreign Policy Research Institute, http://www.fpri.org.

129. Walter Lippmann, "Today and Tomorrow," *New York Herald Tribune*, May 9, 1961.

130. Charles D. Allen and Stephen J. Gerras, "Developing Creative and Critical Thinkers," *Military Review* (November–December 2009), 77–83.

131. Washington's Farewell Address, 1796, cited from The Avalon Project: Documents in Law, History and Diplomacy, Yale Law School's Lillian Goldman Law Library, New Haven, 2008, http://avalon.law.yale.edu.

132. Samuel P. Huntington, *The Clash of Civilizations and the Remaking of World Order*, Simon & Schuster, New York, 1996.

133. This seminar concept derived from groundbreaking work initiated by rules of engagement and use of force experts W. Hays Parks (DoD) and John C. Hall (FBI).

134. JET is an acronym first developed by Captain Mark Kohart, USN, and Commander Thomas Mowell, USN, at the Navy Center for Security Forces, Little Creek, Virginia, after they successfully integrated the ROE/RUF Tactical Training Seminar concept into their program of instruction (POI) for deploying naval forces performing in-lieu-of (ILO) mission in Iraq and Afghanistan.

135. Operation JUMP START, June 2, 2006, rules for force for National Guardsmen on the Southwest Border.

136. Donald Vandergriff, *Military Recruiting: Finding and Preparing Future Soldiers*, citing an interview with Major Andy Dzienwenski, Army National Guard Bureau, April 5, 2008.

137. Donald Vandergriff, *Military Recruiting: Finding and Preparing Future Soldiers*.

138. Ibid., describing the Asymmetric Warfare Group (AWG) located at Fort Meade, Maryland, as originally being founded in 2005 as part of the IED Task Force. It was formally chartered as AWG by the Vice Chief of Staff of the Army in 2006. It takes the latest lessons learned in theaters of operations (war) and helps commanders and staffs translate these lessons into tactics,

techniques, and procedures (TTPs). It has just recently begun teaching the CATC course, which has grown popular within a few short months with units and courses throughout the Army.

139.   Joseph S. Nye Jr., "The Benefits of Soft Power," from "Soft Power and Leadership," *Compass: A Journal of Leadership*, Spring 2004, Center for Public Leadership, John F. Kennedy School of Government, Harvard University.

140.   Thom Shanker, "Defense Secretary Urges More Spending for U.S. Diplomacy," *The New York Times*, December 27, 2007.

141.   Arther Ferrill, *The Fall of the Roman Empire: The Military Explanation*, Thames and Hudson, London, 1986, p. 129.

142.   Department of the Army Form 67-8, Part IV, Section 13.

143.   G. K. Chesterton, "What is Right with the World," *T. P.'s Weekly*, 1910.

144.   Alexandre Havard, *Virtuous Leadership: An Agenda for Personal Excellence*, Scepter Publishers, New York, 2007, p. xvii.

145.   Richard H. Kohn, "Tarnished Brass: Is the U.S. Military Profession in Decline?" *Army History*, Winter 2011, p. 27.

146.   Matt Armstrong, Admiral Mike Mullen on Military Strategy at Kansas State University, March 3, 2010. www.MountainRunner.us

147.   See Qiao Liang and Wang Xiangshui, *Unrestricted Warfare: China's Master Plan to Destroy America*, Natraj Publishing, New Delhi, 2007.

INDEX

Page numbers in italics indicate illustrations.